"I have known Cathy Adams for years, and what I admire most about her is how she infuses everything she does with generosity and care. She is as humble as she is wise. *Zen Parenting* is a beautifully written guide to the parental self-awareness that our kids deserve us to cultivate within ourselves. No matter where you are in your parenting journey, this book will help you bring gentleness and authenticity to yourself and your children."

—ALEXANDRA H. SOLOMON, PHD, LCP, faculty, Northwestern University, bestselling author of *Loving Bravely* and *Taking Sexy Back*

"A sensible, beautiful book, *Zen Parenting* gives parents what we crave most: a reprieve from our near-constant angst and uncertainty. Readers will be comforted by Adams's relatable style, compassionate tone, and brilliant insights. This fresh take on ancient wisdom is so chock-full of fascinating research, I found myself pausing every few pages to text friends a new statistic or data point. A much-needed reminder that good parenting is a practice, not an outcome, *Zen Parenting* is bound to help readers feel more assured, purposeful, and confident even shortly after they begin reading."

—MICHELLE ICARD, author *Fourteen Talks by Age Fourteen*

PRAISE FOR
*ZEN PARENTING*

"*Zen Parenting* gives us the tools to focus on what is truly important as we raise our children. Be curious, accept life's uncertainties, and have the courage to ask yourself hard questions so that you can be the parent you want to be for your child. In a world where parents too often feel unsure, judged, or overwhelmed, *Zen Parenting* gives us a way forward filled with substance and commonsense wisdom. I think this is a wonderful book for any parent!"

—ROSALIND WISEMAN, author of *Queen Bees and Wannabes*, founder of Cultures of Dignity

"Cathy Adams is a gentle, inspiring guide for becoming a more tuned-in, respectful, and connected parent *and* human. What I love most about *Zen Parenting* is Cathy's holistic approach to being present and truly showing up for ourselves and our families, no matter how messy, no matter how challenging. This book is a unique offering in the parenting space that focuses on our relationship with ourselves, which is, of course, where being a Zen parent has to begin."

—DEBBIE REBER, founder Tilt Parenting, author *Differently Wired*

"*Zen Parenting* is not a prescriptive parenting method, it's a guidebook to knowing yourself better so you can be the type of parent your kids need. You'll leave this book with the awareness necessary to disrupt old patterns and build relationships with your kids that will make you proud. It's a wholehearted approach to changing the future of our families for generations to come."

—GEMMA HARTLEY, author of
*Fed Up: Emotional Labor, Women, and the Way Forward*

"*Zen Parenting* offers supportive and empathetic guidance that readers will recognize from the *Zen Parenting* podcast. Drawing from her own experiences with parenting, her mindfulness practice, and her work as a therapist, Cathy Cassani Adams shows us a path to support and nurture our children by understanding ourselves and re-envisioning our daily parenting journey as a practice, not a destination. By diving into our own joys, fears, shame, and longing, and being more observant and curious about our children, we can do a better job empathizing with and supporting our children as they unfold into the fullness of their identities."

—DEVORAH HEITNER, PHD, author of *Screenwise*,
founder of Raising Digital Natives

"*Zen Parenting* takes parents on a journey of self-reflection, but also gives practical tools for how to use that reflection to enhance your parenting. This will be one of the books I recommend to my parents and families."

—MERCEDES SAMUDIO, LCSW, author of
*Shame-Proof Parenting*

# Zen
# Parenting

# Zen Parenting

Understanding Ourselves so we can
Take Better Care of Our Children

**CATHY CASSANI ADAMS, LCSW**

First published in the United States in 2022 by Hachette Go
An imprint of Hachette Books
A division of Hachette Book Group, Inc

First published in Great Britain in 2022 by Yellow Kite
An imprint of Hodder & Stoughton
An Hachette UK company

1

Cover design by Amanda Kain
Interior book design by Jeff Williams
Chakra figure designed by Meghan Lee Design, Graphic Designer

A CIP catalogue record for this title is available from the British Library

Trade Paperback ISBN 978 1 529 36732 4
eBook ISBN 978 1 529 36733 1
Audiobook ISBN 978 1 529 36734 8

Printed and bound in Great Britain by Clays Ltd, Elcograf S.p.A.

Hodder & Stoughton policy is to use papers that are natural, renewable and recyclable products and made from wood grown in sustainable forests. The logging and manufacturing processes are expected to conform to the environmental regulations of the country of origin.

Yellow Kite
Hodder & Stoughton Ltd
Carmelite House
50 Victoria Embankment
London EC4Y 0DZ

www.yellowkitebooks.co.uk

The shape of my life is, of course, determined by many things; my background and childhood, my mind and its education, my conscience and its pressures, my heart and its desires.

—ANNE MORROW LINDBERGH, Gift from the Sea

*For the people who shape my life.*
*Todd, Jacey, Camryn, and Skylar*

# CONTENTS

Prologue: What Is Zen Parenting?    **xv**

    *Where It All Began, xxiii*

Introduction: Foundational Issues to Better
Understand Ourselves, Our Kids, Our World    **1**

    *Emphasizing Dignity, 1*
    *Addressing Inequality, 6*
    *Discussing Race, 9*
    *Prioritizing Sex Education, 16*
    *Understanding Sexuality and Gender, 22*
    *Disrupting Gender Stereotypes and Norms, 25*
    *Valuing Mental Wellness, 36*

Using the Chakra System to Better
Understand Ourselves, Our Kids, Our World    **41**

    *Why Chakras?, 41*
    *Set an Intention, 44*

✿ **CHAKRA ONE**

The Right to Be: Establishing Our Foundation    **49**

    *Body Foundation, 49*
    *Root to Rise, 55*
    *Physical and Emotional Safety, 57*
    *Survival and Connection, 59*
    *Reestablishing Our Roots, 61*

❀ **CHAKRA TWO**

**The Right to Feel: Being Creative,
Accessing Emotions, Experiencing Pleasure**          **67**

*Pleasure, 67*
*Emotional Intelligence, 72*
*Creativity and Play, 79*
*Sexuality, 83*

❀ **CHAKRA THREE**

**The Right to Act:
Establishing Our Identity and Sense of Self**          **93**

*Autonomy and the Hero's Journey, 93*
*Individuation, 96*
*Self-Care, 102*
*Energy, 107*
*True and False Self, 111*

❀ **CHAKRA FOUR**

**The Right to Love and Be Loved:
Loving Ourselves and Others**          **117**

*Openheartedness, 117*
*Empathy, 122*
*Self-Compassion, 128*
*Breathing, 135*
*Grief, 141*

❀ **CHAKRA FIVE**

**The Right to Speak and Hear Truth:
Valuing Authentic Communication**          **151**

*Self-Expression, 151*
*The Art of Communication, 154*
*Words Are Things, 161*
*Heard and Understood, 164*
*Learning Differences, 169*

❄ **CHAKRA SIX**

The Right to See:
Experiencing Our Senses and Intuition　　**177**

*Inner Knowing, 177*
*Truth, 182*
*Mindfulness, 188*
*Meditation, 192*
*Imagination, 198*

❄ **CHAKRA SEVEN**

The Right to Know: Connecting to
Something Greater than Ourselves　　**205**

*Enlightenment, 205*
*Interconnectivity, 208*
*Sacred and Scared, 212*
*Devotion, 214*

Conclusion　　　　221
Acknowledgments　　227
Appendix　　　　　229
Notes　　　　　　235

# PROLOGUE

## *What Is Zen Parenting?*

Trying to describe Zen can cause it to lose its meaning entirely. Knowing this, old masters would just say, "Zen is Zen," as if that would offer some type of clarity to their students. What they knew is that trying to define or hold the meaning of Zen drives us further from it, and by reducing it to words, it is no longer Zen, similar to the understanding of the first chapter of the *Tao Te Ching*:

> *The tao is beyond words*
> *and beyond understanding*
> *Words may be used to speak of it,*
> *but they cannot contain it.*[1]

This word puzzle points to the fact that a word like *Zen* cannot be easily defined, and while it's often used to describe being chill or relaxed, that doesn't encapsulate its meaning. Zen points to an *intangible and paradoxical appreciation of the uncertainty of our lives*, and I use the word *points* because it doesn't offer specific steps or offer an absolute understanding. It demands that we appreciate and embrace what we are experiencing while living in the uncertainty of not knowing, like when a Zen teacher was handed a teacup and said, "Knowing this glass is fragile, and will break if I drop it, I can fully appreciate and enjoy the beauty of the glass as I hold it carefully."[2] Once we respect the impermanence and ever-changing aspects of life, we can be present enough to flow with it rather than try to control it.

Zen is about showing up for every aspect of life, the joy and the pain. It's about observing instead of turning away and accepting rather than rejecting. It's about finding value in what we tend to label both "good" and "bad" and appreciating the humor in my favorite quote from Zen monk Shunryu Suzuki, "Each of you is perfect the way you are . . . and you can use a little improvement."[3]

In traditional Chinese philosophy, the yin-yang symbol is used to demonstrate the duality of male-female, light-dark, peace-war. All seemingly opposite characteristics are complementary and interdependent, represented by the yin-yang symbol having a dot of the opposite color inside of it. Generally speaking, yin is characterized as an inward energy that is feminine, still, and dark, and yang is characterized as outward energy, masculine, hot, and bright. It speaks to how our world and lives are composed of different and often opposing forces that coexist and even complement each other. Forces opposite each other even come to rely on one another to exist; as there is no shadow without light, there is no death without life.

This is why my husband and I chose a yin-yang symbol to represent our *Zen Parenting Radio* podcast, because duality lives at the heart of all of our discussions. How do we embrace the ambiguity and ever-changing nature of life and still live with an open mind and heart? Even our original *Zen Parenting Radio* podcast tagline—*A logical practical dad and an emotional and spiritual mom discuss parenting*—speaks to the value of two often contradictory perspectives living in harmony.

The word *Zen* in this book and for the *Zen Parenting Radio* podcast is used not to claim a lifelong study with a master or as a religious path, but as the word that best captures the uncertain and ever-changing human experience. With deep regard for its roots and what the word is attempting to capture, we understand ourselves to be lifelong students of its meaning. Zen represents attentive evolving, and we do our best to approach it as *the nature of self-awareness, as a deeper understanding of ourselves and others through repeated and consistent practice.*

Zen also points to a tolerance for ambiguity and becoming comfortable with paradox, like *we only change when we accept who we are* or *the more we try to control, the less control we will have.* These contradictions induce what Carl Jung called a "mental cramp," the challenge we feel when we begin to confront our unconscious workings.

Jung also believed that paradox offered more justice to the unknowable than clarity could, an understanding that paradox allows us to see the whole by holding the tension of opposites.

The truth always lies somewhere in between, and paradox protects us from thinking we have all the answers by reminding us how many things can be true at once. *We notice the beauty in the midst of pain; we take things seriously while laughing at the absurdity.* This is how we can see and understand ourselves more clearly and then see and understand our partners and children with more willing and open minds.

It's also paradoxical that if you start calling yourself a Zen Parent, you've already lost the point. The word is best used to help us stand back and notice rather than define who we are. It's not a label or prescriptive way to parent, but a willingness to stay present in what's happening and engaging in life as it is. Spiritual author Richard Rohr explains this human engagement in three cyclical stages—*order, disorder, and reorder*—and parenting can be explained and experienced the same way.

The one thing that can be counted on throughout parenting is change—just when we understand our child's experience or buy the right-size clothes, they change and grow. Just when we get comfortable with typical life challenges, the world experiences a global pandemic. Being able to parent and live well requires a willingness to get comfortable with disorder and uncertainty and even more of a willingness to be introspective and creative to once again find reorder.

Zen Parenting necessitates that we take responsibility for our energy so we can attend to ourselves and our children in the present time. It's a commitment to an imperfect practice of continual self-awareness so we can show up in the most authentic and mindful way. Instead of a scripted life, it's a moment-to-moment experience of what's in front of us. We drop our expectations and do right now.

The tagline from our *Zen Parenting Radio* podcast comes from Dr. Dan Siegel: "The best predictor of a child's well-being is a parent's self-understanding." To raise a child well, it's most important to continually raise and parent ourselves first, to recognize the energy we bring to every situation, to be clear about the "why" behind all of the expectations we have for our children.

That means that everything starts with us: why we believe what we believe, why we say what we say, and how well we see and understand the stories that live behind our feelings and actions. Instead of looking at our kids and expecting them to play out the life we have choreographed, we first look at ourselves and figure out where we came up with the choreography.

We may be perpetuating beliefs that were imposed on our grandparents, parents, then us—a continuous cycle of unexamined expectation. We may be preserving a certain way of living or thinking that is actually no longer relevant to this time and place. We may be making choices and decisions to please people who are no longer here or continually chasing a dream that was never ours.

Self-awareness means noticing whatever script we were handed by our family, religion, or society and questioning whether it works for us. It may have had good intention or necessity for a certain time, but it may be stifling or harming us in the present time. It may be suffocating our sense of self, damaging our partnerships, or disconnecting us from our children.

Pain and struggle are wake-up calls, opportunities to be broken open and figure out how to put ourselves back together in a more authentic way, to release the parts that were imposed on us and discover the parts that we may have safely hidden. It's an ongoing process, not a onetime experience, and we begin to experience and accept it as the natural ebb and flow of life. Instead of holding on too tight, we practice loosening the grip and expanding what we conceive as possible.

Zen Parenting means humility and a broader perspective that's less about answers and more about living the questions. It demands that we honor and access all of our emotions, to know that all of them play a role in directing us where we need to go. We learn that there is strength in vulnerability and that there is a necessity in getting comfortable with the uncomfortable. This acceptance decreases our need to be defensive or righteous and allows us to open ourselves to listening and learning.

We will inevitably make mistakes, and growth and wisdom come from our ability to accept our humanness and make adjustments along the way. Life is inherently unpredictable. We will all suffer disappointment and pain, but we can trust our hardwiring for challenge and resilience, to experience ourselves as part of something bigger as we maneuver through what's difficult.

A lot of my therapy clients have acquired all the things they thought they wanted—marriage, kids, a house, work—yet they still feel deeply unhappy and lonely. They live with people and spend time in crowded rooms, yet they still feel isolated. This is because they are disconnected from themselves and their external lives do not match up with their internal desires. They feel the pressure of *must* rather than the opportunity to *choose*. Parenting from this place creates a cycle of disconnection that disrupts how we experience our kids and how our kids will inevitably experience us.

Self-awareness that leads to self-acceptance are the things we're always searching for, the holes and gaps we are always trying to fill. The happy pictures on Instagram are filled with external pleasures and things we're taught to reach for: money, vacations, clothes, beauty. And while these things can indeed be pleasurable, they can also turn into a bottomless pit of needing more. Peace and contentment depend on an internal investigation and individual practice that lead to self-acceptance.

Then we can notice and quiet the running tape of self-criticisms and "shoulds" in our mind so we can stay present and lead from our more intuitive selves. The practice of self-awareness brings us back to who we are and develops our empathy and understanding of others, an ongoing process that brings us closer to center.

Once we experience what it feels like to let go of expectations, pressure, and falseness, we can offer this freedom to our kids. We can allow them to grow up with a sense of self where they don't have to learn all of the things we are still trying to unlearn. We can help them ground themselves in purpose and belonging so they can live with self-trust and connection to the world.

This book is for you so you can experience the joy that's your birthright and so you can answer the question that Mary Oliver posed: "Tell me, what is it you plan to do with your one wild and precious life?"[4]

**Knowing and inhabiting your answer will keep you from giving your children their answer. You will know who you are, and then you can set your kids free to become who they are.** Your relationship with them will be about support and acceptance rather than societal expectation.

Zen Parenting is about reframing our personal and parenting experiences. It is a personal interrogation and a moment-to-moment practice of locating ourselves so we can be here now. Here is the only place our children can feel us; now is the only thing that's real.

## Where It All Began

It was 1998, and I was watching Madonna talk about her just-released *Ray of Light* album. She said the songs were about her spiritual transformation, an evolution of her sound that gave her purpose and perspective about who she is and what she wanted to teach her daughter.

I didn't have kids yet, and I wasn't married, but I nodded my head as if I heard something I already knew. We have to know ourselves if we want to live and parent effectively; we can't share what we haven't realized or practiced.

I might have known this intuitively, or maybe all of the self-help books had begun to seep in. I read my first Wayne Dyer book in my late teens, and from then on I had a gravitational pull to the self-help and positive-psychology aisle. But at best I was using the information as a quick fix, and at worst I was acquiring spiritual knowledge to feel special. It was only a surface experience with consciousness and universal principles. I liked the way it felt and sounded, but I wasn't living what I knew.

And then a series of life-changing events, including my father's heart attack and chronic illness, getting married, and eventually having my first child, pushed me into deep discomfort. What had always worked was no longer working, and this led to an identity crisis and a heightened sense of impostor syndrome. I felt increasingly depressed and anxious, so much so that I was willing to surrender everything for peace. It was my Madonna *Ray of Light* moment—I had to break down the structures I had relied on to discover a true way of being.

Some refer to this as *the dark night of the soul*, but, unfortunately, it extends beyond one night. It's a deep dive into a new way of seeing things when the old ways no longer work, a revaluation of what's most important. At the time I called it a personal reckoning, a reconciliation of pain that had been denied or repressed and an unlearning of things that no longer worked.

The best way I can describe the first couple years of this process is **yikes**. The unexamined life felt like a *much* easier path, and I often questioned what the hell I was doing. Confronting the truth about anything can be painful and difficult, and I constantly wondered if the road less traveled was worth it.

But with pain and unlearning also come clarity of choices and a focus on what really matters. Life felt like more about finding my own contentment rather than satisfying other people's expectations. I said no to what didn't work; I said yes to what I knew I wanted. I started to feel more comfortable in my skin and connected to what was happening around me. *My sole intention was to continuously locate the person I was before the world told me to be something different.*

I remember at one point fully comprehending that we live on a ball floating in space surrounded by two trillion galaxies and that maybe the things that seemed so overwhelming weren't that important. It literally made me shake my head and laugh out loud, like I was finding my way back to the bigger picture. Being a part of it all blew my mind, and Rumi's quote "You are the universe in ec-static motion" made sense in a new way.[5]

I was suddenly in awe that babies grew in our bodies and needed no help in doing so, that caterpillars become goo and then turn into butterflies, that salmon use their sense of smell to swim upstream. Things that had seemed so common now felt extraordinary, like life had a natural rhythm and sense of purpose.

It became obvious that I needed to make peace with the mortality of my dad and just death overall. Death is what all living things have in common, yet we are so un-comfortable talking about it. As author and Zen Hospice founder Frank Ostaseski said, "Death is not waiting for us at the end of a long road. Death is always with us, in the marrow of every passing moment. She is the secret teacher hiding in plain sight, helping us to discover what matters most."[6]

Death awareness leads to appreciating life's precious-ness, encouraging us to be braver and more attentive with our lives. The more I got this, the more I enjoyed staring out windows rather than at my computer screen. I took some risks talking, writing, and teaching what I was learn-ing, and I made some mistakes along the way. I remem-ber one of my teachers saying, "Keep making mistakes, because if there are no more mistakes, you are done—and I don't mean done with that thing, I mean done, done."

It felt like permission to go all in with less worry, like raising my hand to ask a question rather than pretending I understood.

But since there are light and dark to everything, old beliefs still lurked in my brain like old ghosts that knew only how to be scary. They would frighten me into thinking that if I continued to unlearn or grew in self-awareness, I might end up leaving my family and living as a monk on a mountaintop. This was a *real* concern that kept me up at night, a feeling that I was choosing myself over others, that I was selfish or losing touch with the "real" world.

I later learned that a lot of women feel this way as they awaken to themselves. It's as if we feel the collective unconsciousness of all women, the historical reality that women were confronted with the terror and risk of evolving beyond their societal conditioning, not because of weakness or a lack of desire, but because of the threat of societal isolation, retribution, or death. Evolving today may not carry the same risks as our ancestors, but it's still a level of awareness that all women must move through, a realization that awake women disturb the system and that this disruption is a threat to our conditioned self and society as a whole. Something needs to die for something new to come to life.

But once we hear (feel, however we experience it) the call to evolve, it can be difficult or almost impossible to turn down its volume. Trying to stay asleep—and believe me, I tried—made me physically and emotionally ill, and I no longer had the choice to push it away. I felt compelled by something larger than myself, leaving me terrified and relieved at the same time. As Sue Monk Kidd says in *The Dance of the Dissident Daughter*, "There is no place so awake and alive as the edge of becoming. But more than that, birthing the kind of woman who can authentically say, 'My soul is my own,' and then embody it in her life, her spirituality, and her community is worth the risk and hardship."[7]

I continued to learn and grow, but the terror stuck around, telling me I would change and become unrecognizable to myself and the ones I love. But in many ways, the result was quite the opposite. I did have to grieve some relationships and work experiences that no longer fit with my new understanding, but I also had more energy to show up for my family. Taking responsibility for myself let the people I loved off the hook; it was no longer their responsibility to fill me up, and I no longer felt like I was in charge of their becoming.

I experienced the paradox of loving them better by backing away, by living my life so they could have their own. I set myself free from needing their constant appreciation and then felt more appreciated. I ditched the "role" of mom and became a person who also happened to *be* a mom, which allowed me to approach my kids with humanness rather than hierarchy. I got out of the box that told me who I was supposed to be and showed up as myself, allowing me to show up more authentically for my family.

Self-awareness is an internal process, like shining a bright flashlight on all the hidden places of the mind. This ability to see clearly allows us to know ourselves and appreciate who we are, allowing us to choose rather than react and trust rather than live in a constant state of anxiety. Shit still happens, but the lag time of feeling fear and pain gets shorter, while the ability to return to center or ask for help speeds up.

If we can role model and teach our kids how to see themselves clearly from the very beginning, the flashlight won't be as needed because they'll already have a working light switch. They can naturally check in with their emotions and appreciate why they have them. They can use tools to self-regulate rather than spiral into a tantrum. They can appreciate the uniqueness of their minds and hearts and live in a place of self-acceptance rather than shame.

Education and outward achievement are pieces of the "good life" puzzle, but true contentment comes from a healthy internal life. Study after study has proven that emotional intelligence (defined as the ability to recognize, understand, and manage our own emotions and recognize, understand, and influence the emotions of others) predicts future success in relationships, health, and quality of life and that children with high EQ earn better grades, stay in school longer, and make healthier choices overall.

Instead of forcing kids into what we perceive to be the norm, we can teach them to respect their uniqueness and practice self-compassion during difficult times. We can remind them they are hardwired for challenges and that even failure will lead to greater strength and resilience. We can encourage them to love their time here, to show up as themselves and take advantage of their moments.

If we want our kids to *really* get this, we must do it first. Instead of lecturing them about self-acceptance, we need to demonstrate what it looks like. Instead of telling them to ask for help or for what they need, we need to show them how it's done. Children do not learn by listening to what we say; they learn by watching how we live.

This book is about having your Madonna *Ray of Light* moment, about practicing self-awareness to gain clarity about what you want to pass on. It's about taking inventory of how you were parented and figuring out what stays and what goes. This is a needed evolutionary process that is essential for every generation because the world and level of awareness are constantly changing. Some traditions and expectations will remain timeless, but other teachings or expectations may no longer fit. If your children have children, they will hopefully go through the same exercise of filtering through what works and what doesn't for their family.

This is also an opportunity to introduce yourself to your kids: to be your true self as a parent rather than play the "role" of parent, to support your kids without completely forgetting who you are or choosing martyrdom and then wearing it like a badge of honor. Martyrdom hurts you and eventually your family because it leads to your resenting them for what you do. You build a relationship with your kids over time, and it's important to establish a sturdy foundation built on personal responsibility and practicing what you preach.

Sitting on the sidelines of life and then yelling at our kids about how they should participate isn't fair and will inevitably lead to tension and disconnection. Instead, we get to demonstrate self-understanding and self-compassion; we get to recognize our mistakes and apologize when necessary. We get to notice and accept our emotions and trust that they will naturally come and go. We get to be joy seekers and expand our awareness so we can see the big picture and interconnectedness of all things. Then our kids will know how to be awed by the world and feel at home in their skin, wherever they may go.

# INTRODUCTION

*Foundational Issues to Better Understand
Ourselves, Our Kids, Our World*

## Emphasizing Dignity

Dignity is as essential to human life as water,
food, and oxygen.

—LAURA HILLENBRAND, Unbroken: An Extraordinary
True Story of Courage and Survival

Our friend Rosalind Wiseman, author of *Queen Bees and
Wannabes*, started an organization with the absolute best
name—**Cultures of Dignity**. I told her how much I loved it
and that I think it sums up everything we need to be teaching and understanding. She responded by saying, "I think
it's our way back to each other."

One of the most important distinctions in her organization is the difference between respect and dignity. Respect

is something *earned* through what you have achieved and how you have handled yourself as you've achieved. Dignity is *given*, and no one can take it away. All people should be treated ethically with reverence for their inherent humanity, including all children.

This definition and understanding are the keys to reflective and respectful discourse, the way we can relate to ourselves and each other. We may not respect what or how someone has achieved, but we don't have permission to treat anyone in a way that is cruel or condescending, including ourselves.

We may look through our past with embarrassment or regret, but our dignity can remain. It can serve as our foundation for change, what we rely on to forge a new path. We may need to atone for what we have done or accept the consequences of our behavior, but dignity is inherent.

Once we believe this for ourselves, we offer it to others. We can disagree with someone without tearing them down. We can choose to part ways with someone without smearing their name. We can understand why a person's pain may lead them to make poor choices or project what they feel. We become willing to see a whole person rather than just a behavior.

Reflective and respectful discourse relies on a person knowing their inherent worth and the inherent worth of others. A person needs to feel grounded enough to share their beliefs while staying open to new ideas. Too often we share our beliefs with righteousness, believing that if someone disagrees, they are disrespecting us or questioning us as a person. It's a defensiveness that comes from shame or a lack of self-trust; not believing in our inherent dignity and worth causes us to react from insecurity and blame others for what we feel.

When two people do this, it's close to impossible to converse or connect. Conversations become about winning or losing rather than hearing and learning. If we grew up witnessing or experiencing this type of communication, we may do it on autopilot. We may not even realize that discussions can be safe and satisfying rather than defensive or toxic.

**As parents we need to work on embracing our dignity so we can offer the same to our children. Our most important work as parents is to notice and take care of ourselves, to recognize our patterns and habits and take responsibility for what's ours rather than blame others.** If we don't, it will inevitably affect the communication and relationship with our children.

If our children have a different perspective, we may immediately view them as disrespectful. If they ask questions, we perceive it as "talking back." If they share their frustration, we may call them "sassy," and if they share their emotions, we may call them "dramatic." Being constantly triggered and offended by our children may be an indicator that we have our own unrecognized or unresolved pain.

A lot of my clients, mostly women, spent their childhoods or young adult lives not feeling seen or understood. Not feeling seen or heard in the past can dictate how we respond to our children's inability to follow directions in the present. We may ask a child to put their shoes away, and if they don't we find ourselves yelling or reacting intensely.

The child not listening triggers past feelings of being unheard, and the child is held accountable for things that have nothing to do with them. Of course, we would all like our children to listen the first time and put their shoes away, but an intense overreaction to their inability to do so is often connected to a history we haven't fully processed.

This can also be true at work or in our partnership, and it's our responsibility to recognize these overreactions and question their origins. If we can't remember a specific trauma or situation, can we notice an underlying feeling or belief that we carry, like not being good enough or not feeling valued or seen? This awareness can be the beginning of unlearning, of a willingness to question an outdated or false belief system.

Then we can show up for present-day conversations with self-awareness and willingness to listen rather than react and defend. We can get feedback without feeling we need to retaliate; we can ask questions without feeling less than. This is the beginning of reflective and respectful discourse, and it's the practice that Todd and I do our best to model on our *Zen Parenting Radio* podcast.

Todd and I don't agree on everything; in fact, we tend to experience the world very differently. He is more pragmatic; I am more spiritual. He is an extrovert; I am an introvert. But we get constant opportunities to practice communicating with a sense of self-awareness and accountability, noticing ourselves as we speak and listen so we can stay connected and learn.

We get triggered and frustrated—there is no way to completely avoid these experiences—but instead of going what we call "primitive" and getting lost in our reptilian brain of fight or flight, we do our best to stay in the more rational prefrontal cortex of our brain so we can choose to breathe instead of walk away or get curious rather than retaliate. Then we can take responsibility for our feelings and insecurities so we don't project them onto each other. We also use humor (respectfully, not at each other's expense) to defuse a situation, and we are willing to apologize if we have crossed the line.

Practicing with each other allows us to communicate in a similar way with our kids. Mistakes are made, but we know we can take responsibility and start again. It's not about eliminating challenges; it's about knowing we can handle the challenges in a dignified and self-aware manner.

Rob Bell was the keynote at our 2017 Zen Parenting Conference, and during his talk he jokingly said to the teenagers in the audience, "If your parents are really coming at you, you should ask them, 'Is this mine, or is this yours?'" This received a lot of knowing laughter because a lot of the frustration we project on our kids is about us: our history, our day at work, our frustration at ourselves, our frustration that our children aren't doing what *we* think they should be doing.

And while there are safety matters that are nonnegotiable, our children's life choices really belong to them.

We may have to let go of how we thought it would be so they can become who they are; they take the lead, and we show up as a guide and support system. Then we get the privilege of knowing them, of being connected now while building and sustaining a relationship for a lifetime.

## Addressing Inequality

> The good we secure for ourselves is precarious and uncertain, is floating in mid-air, until it is secured for all of us and incorporated into our common life.
>
> —JANE ADDAMS, *"The Subjective Necessity for Social Settlements," lecture, School of Applied Ethics, Plymouth, Massachusetts, July 1, 1892*

We are a society built on default settings of the majority experience, causing us to ignore or stay silent about things we don't experience or can't personally relate to. Some of us recognize injustices early in our lives and actively become an ally or advocate for equality, but many of us use our privilege to go about our lives without considering disparity. Parenting can be yet another wake-up call to notice how our systems and communities are unfairly structured, urging us to pay attention so we can address inequalities with our children.

This necessitates a willingness to recognize our own blind spots when it comes to issues of equality, to investigate what we've been taught and parse out what continues to be harmful. Even if we were raised in an open-minded and progressive family, we need to remain students when it comes to other people's lived experiences. And no matter the positive intention of our family or community, we can recognize that judgments and prejudice originate from a society built around systematized oppression, increasing the urgency for us to dig deep and notice what we may have consciously or unconsciously internalized.

Gaining a new perspective means we have to be willing to listen, to be conscious of our ego's resistance and need to be right. We have to work on dismantling all types of prejudice within ourselves, which can be quite messy and uncomfortable, with expected mistakes and missteps. As Ijeoma Oluo says in *So You Want to Talk About Race*, "You have to get over the fear of facing the worst in yourself. You should instead fear unexamined racism. Fear the thought that right now, you could be contributing to the oppression of others and you don't know it. But do not fear those who bring that oppression to light. Do not fear the opportunity to do better."[1]

Parents constantly tell me that they want to raise their kids in a more peaceful world, but these same parents have difficulty recognizing what this means in regard to their own self-awareness. Nelson Mandela said, "The first thing is to be honest with yourself. You can never have an impact on society if you have not changed yourself. . . . Great peacemakers are all people of integrity, of honesty, but humility."[2]

To be peacemakers in our homes, we need to lead with humility and a desire to learn and grow. An unwillingness to investigate ourselves and our privilege leads to arrogance, allowing us to point our finger at others as we stay quiet and uninterested in becoming part of a solution. Groups that experience oppression do not have the luxury of being uninterested and are forced to fight for their rights. They are often blamed for what they didn't create and put in a position of convincing the majority that they are worthy of what others expect to receive.

We shy away from learning more due to shame and what we have or haven't done, but the more educated we become about other people's experiences, the more we tap into the inherent dignity of all people. True connection necessitates listening and learning, setting the stage for dismantling and unlearning harmful ideology that lives inside of us and our culture. As parents, it's our responsibility to raise citizens of the world, which means honoring the dignity of all people by educating ourselves and our children when it comes to differences and equality.

Pay attention to subjects that feel undiscussable, because feeling undiscussable may cause you to tuck them away as bad or shameful, increasing the likelihood of misunderstandings or false beliefs. Topics such as ableism, deformities or facial differences, poverty, learning disabilities, religion, finances, and other societal issues are not primary discussions in this book, but if any of them show up in your life and feel undiscussable, it would be wise to explore when and how they became off-limits.

On Brené Brown's *Unlocking Us* podcast, actor Mark Duplass wisely said that "the truth is hard, but it's so much easier."[3] Telling the truth and talking openly about things early and often can be uncomfortable, but it's so much easier than attempting to dismantle misinformation about things that have been avoided.

Issues of inequality are never simple and are often controversial, but that makes them more important to interrogate within ourselves and figure out how to discuss them with our kids. Avoiding these topics does not keep our kids from having to deal with them; it only makes them less astute in understanding and conversing about the very real issues of their world.

## Discussing Race

> Racism is a reality that so many of us grow up learning to just deal with. But if we ever hope to move past it, it can't just be on people of color to deal with it. It's up to all of us—Black, white, everyone—no matter how well-meaning we think we might be, to do the honest, uncomfortable work of rooting it out.
>
> —MICHELLE OBAMA (@MICHELLEOBAMA),
> *Twitter, May 29, 2020*

People of color can easily see the systemic racism that has affected their lives; their everyday experiences and family histories reflect the disproportionate power structures that are at the foundation of our country. It can be difficult for white people to recognize and acknowledge how the current system is set up in their favor. Socioeconomic disparity and traumatic experiences may increase the struggle for someone who is white, but being a person of color, especially a person of color whose history is based in slavery or being forced from their homeland by the government, is not a struggle that white people face. As Isabel Wilkerson says in *Caste*, "Radical empathy means putting in the work to educate oneself and to listen with a humble heart to understand another's experience from their perspective, not as we imagine we would feel. Radical empathy is not about you and what you think you would do in a situation you have never been in and perhaps never will. It is the kindred connection from a place of deep knowing that opens your spirit to the pain of another as they perceive it."[4]

Caryn Park, a researcher at Antioch University in Seattle who focuses on children's understanding of race and ethnicity, says that children as young as three years old are aware of and interested in race and skin color. Park says, "Their identities really matter to them, and racial identity is a significant part of their total identity. They also understand the power in talking about race and racism, and that when they bring those things up, they can get the attention of grown-ups and other children."[5]

Author Ibram X. Kendi says the goal is to raise children who are *antiracist*, explaining, "We should raise children who can express notions of racial equality, who can see racial disparities as a problem, and who can do their own small part to challenge this big problem of racism."[6] This means first recognizing racist ideas that we as parents may have internalized, unintentionally or not, and begin our own unlearning process. It's our job to recognize what we believe and where we learned it while staying open to a more honest way of seeing differences.

It's vital to become educated about our country's history when it comes to race. We need to seek out diverse teachers, authors, and thought leaders who offer a more accurate depiction of our history so we don't continue to pass along outdated ideology that is harmful to our children, other people's children, and society as a whole. Opening up communication about race gives our kids the ability to respect differences and become conscious of the trappings of prejudice and racism.

Most of my experiences as an educator have been with the Latino community, starting in my early twenties as a teacher in a migrant education program run by my father, then as an educator teaching English as a second language for frontline employees, and for the past ten years in the Sociology/Criminology Department of Dominican University, where the students are predominantly Hispanic. Even with my experience, I am consistently educated about the ever-changing nature of the community, including the words chosen to reference it. There has been a shift from *Hispanic* to *Latino/Latina*, to now *Latinx*, which is still not universally used and up for debate. The Pew Research Center did a national survey of Latinos in 2020 and found that only one in four has heard the term *Latinx*, only 3 percent use it, and the majority who use it are eighteen to twenty-nine years old.[7] Even the pronunciation of *Latinx* can differ. My students pronounce the word *Latin-x*, but I still hear *La-teen-x* used when listening to others.

It's less about perfect agreement and more about the ongoing conversation, so every semester I ask my students to share the preferred language when addressing their community, and I follow their lead. We confront and discuss the ever-changing nature of their community, especially when it comes to immigration and the looming threat of deportation of their undocumented family members. To talk about immigration and deportation without knowing the people who are affected is to be blind to the deep suffering that is caused. The increase in fear and anxiety of my students after the 2016 election was palpable and a constant topic of conversation, and a large percentage of their final presentations since 2016 have focused around the injustices surrounding immigration and detainment and how this personally affects them and their families.

They share injustices when it comes to law enforcement within their community and how they are targeted and treated poorly within the system. Their experiences are often the reason they end up in my social work class, because they are interested in becoming part of the solution. Many of my students plan on becoming police officers, juvenile advocates, lawyers, border patrol agents, social workers, and mental health professionals to reform what they know firsthand is unfair.

Most of my students work full- or part-time to pay for their education and help support their families. Their support is not limited to finances: some are expected to care for siblings and cousins or for aging or ailing parents and grandparents. Their bilingualism often puts them front and center if their family is navigating the educational and legal systems or any other system that is difficult even for a native English speaker.

Even with all this pressure and expectation, the majority of my students are stellar athletes, activists, and leaders within the school, while also being mentors or leaders in their churches or focusing on outreach and crime deterrence within their own neighborhoods. Most of them consider themselves privileged because they are often the first generation in their family to attend college. Yet this has a pressure all its own, carrying an expectation that they will break through in ways that other family members have found impossible.

My experience with this community, and the other communities of color that I've been privileged to work with, was paramount in my choosing social work as a profession. The National Association of Social Workers Code of Ethics stresses standing up for social justice, respecting the dignity and inherent worth of all people, and paying attention to the importance of human relationships. Ideally, this would be the expectation of all and not the work of some. Social work done right is not just a job; it's a viewpoint that evolves your thinking and how you experience and interact with people. Differences are seen and respected, but the walls between us are always false. We are always each other.

If we do not have close or personal experience with people of different races, we too easily fall back on media depictions or stereotypes, never really relating because we are not close enough to engage in the full humanity of others. Racial identification is not a unified force or monolith; the differences between people and communities are vast and deep, with gender, religion, socioeconomic status, political ideology, and educational attainment all playing a role. Bryan Stevenson, founder and executive director of the Equal Justice Initiative, suggests being more "proximate" to understand the nuanced experiences of those who experience inequality. He says, "Proximity is a pathway through which we learn the kind of things we need to know to make healthier communities."[8]

As parents we can begin to harness a better understanding through proximity, education, and talking openly about race and equal treatment of all people. We can do this not just through lecture but also through our actions and readiness to take a stand on issues that are unequal or unjust. It's an ongoing practice of monitoring and paying attention to old patterns of thought so we don't fall back into ignorance or silence. As author Austin Channing Brown says in *I'm Still Here: Black Dignity in a World Made for Whiteness*, "The march toward change has been grueling, but it is real. And all it has ever taken was the transformed—the people of color confronting past and present to imagine a new future, and the handful of white people willing to release indifference and join the struggle."[9]

Kids who develop empathy, compassion, and a sense of justice at an early age become adults who strive for awareness and equality, which means talking about racism should begin early and remain an ongoing family discussion. There should be space and time to talk about news events and allow for questions, which means parents need to be educated about the history of race relations and race-based current events.

Unfortunately, studies have shown that white parents rarely engage their kids in race conversations. In a 2012 study, mothers were videotaped reading a race-themed book to their four- and five-year-olds, and 94 percent of the mothers read the book "without making any comments about race or ethnicity, diversity, or intergroup contact." Even if the kids asked specific questions about race, the mothers mostly avoided answering or simply alluded to race, through comments like "We should treat everyone equally" or "Even if we look different, we're all the same on the inside."[10]

A study published in 2011 asked parents to discuss race with their five- to seven-year-old white kids over the course of a week, and the kids who had these conversations with their parents showed less racial bias than the kids who didn't.[11]

Our willingness to have discussions makes an impact, and our ability to supplement open discussion with books and movies that center people of color allows our children to experience plenty of diverse protagonists who experience challenges but also common, everyday joy. Having a diverse range of movies, television shows, and books, as well as other media and tech, is powerful and makes a big impression. The media we choose and the conversations they create allow for ongoing learning that intensifies as our children age. We can create space and time to speak up and amplify issues of inequity and injustice so our children experience allyship as an expected part of world engagement.

## Prioritizing Sex Education

> Sex education, including its spiritual aspects, should be part of a broad health and moral education from kindergarten through grade twelve, ideally carried out harmoniously by parents and teachers.
>
> —DR. BENJAMIN SPOCK,
> Dr. Spock's Baby and Child Care

Just like learning how to play or talk, sex education is a fundamental part of our human development. We shy away from discussions mostly because many of us grew up at a time when talking about these things was uncommon. It is in the best interest of our children's health to talk about sexuality and gender early and often, but lacking a model to follow, we mimic our parents by doing the bare minimum. These are usually the parents who say, "I turned out okay, and nobody talked to me about sex . . . ," yet they are currently sitting in my office talking to me about their issues with sex.

We can make a choice to become more aware of what we needed when we were young and begin to educate ourselves about sex, specifically unlearning the shame and pain we may have accumulated or inherited as children.

As Dr. Daniel Siegel says in *The Whole-Brain Child*, "When neurons fire together, they grow new connections between them." Or said simply by neuropsychologist Donald Hebb, "Neurons that fire together, wire together."[12] If sex is taught with guilt and shame, the brain's neurons will entwine sex with shame. If it is taught with awareness and comfort, the brain will entwine sex with standard human behavior.

Sex is not just about the act of sex; it's more about what it means to experience our human bodies, relationships, and communities. This is best demonstrated through comprehensive sexuality education (CSE), which seeks to "equip young people with the knowledge, skills, attitudes and values they need to determine and enjoy their sexuality—physically and emotionally, individually and in relationships. It views sexuality holistically, as a part of young people's emotional and social development. It recognizes that information alone is not enough. Young people need to be given the opportunity to acquire essential life skills and develop positive attitudes and values."[13]

While CSE is well researched and backed by a number of health associations and child welfare groups, there is still pushback about how talking early and often about sex and gender robs children of their "innocence."

Author Bonnie Rough speaks to this issue in her book *Beyond Birds & Bees*, where she focuses on her experiences living in Amsterdam, where sexuality and gender are addressed openly, leading to much better outcomes when it comes to pregnancy, sexually transmitted diseases, and overall self-acceptance and happiness within relationships. She says, "Innocence. Here was the heart of the matter. As a culture, we Americans cherish children. We say revere the 'sanctity of childhood.' And despite the fact that even in America things used to be more open, sex education over the past half century has gained a sinister reputation."[14]

She goes on to explain that "guarding" children from knowledge about their own bodies and the nature of relationships actually has the opposite effect, that open communication and receptivity to children's questions does not derail childhood, but leads to a child feeling more secure, connected, and comfortable in their skin. Even Focus on the Family, a conservative fundamentalist Christian organization, has in boldface type on their website, "Giving a child facts about reproduction, including details about intercourse, does not rob him of innocence. Innocence is a function of attitude, not information."[15]

Sex is sexual activity, including specifically sexual intercourse, but it's not just the acts of sex that need to be explained and discussed. Sexual feelings, decisions, and outcomes need to be in the mix, because it's the feelings and decisions that lead to the acts. Parents often avoid these conversations out of fear of not having the right answers, saying too much, or discovering something they don't want to know about their child.

Most parents I work with tend to avoid discussing sex with their children because of their overall discomfort or shame about their own sexual choices when they were young. I work with individual clients and offer sex-education presentations to parents to relieve some of the discomfort so they can offer their kids something healthier or more productive. The hope is that this leads to an ongoing, continuous effort to pay attention to how we respond to our children and question anything that keeps us quiet or shut down when it comes to sex.

I also teach sex education to fifth and eighth graders, and I can tell you that these kids and young adults want and need information. If parents do not show up for these discussions, peers will take on the role of teachers, and the peers who are the loudest often have the most incorrect and detrimental information. I am most dismayed when teens tell me that sex acts are "no big deal," or they feel that to keep a relationship they must be sexually active before they feel ready, or they spend their days feeling disconnected or disgusted by their own bodies.

I am also bummed when I work with fifth grade girls who have never heard of a period, who feel ashamed of their growing curiosity, and who think that anything about their developing body is inherently "gross." While I meet plenty of young and older girls who have a positive understanding of their body and their sexuality, the majority of young girls I work with cover their faces, close their ears, and laugh to hide their discomfort when I talk about body parts or normal feelings while going through puberty. Too many fifth and eighth grade girls have told me that I am the first adult who has ever talked to them about their bodies or sex, and because I'm there only once a year for maybe two hours tops, this demonstrates a challenge when it comes to developing a healthy sense of self.

School sex-education programs are important and necessary, but they are only supplemental to an ongoing conversation that needs to be had at home. Young kids need to understand how their bodies work and need to know that if they have questions, someone is willing to answer. As a parent, it's not about having perfect answers or one big talk; it's about allowing for questions and ongoing conversation so a child can normalize the experience of their developing body and mind.

I often ask parents to envision what they want for their kids when it comes to sex, and the vast majority say they want their children to mature into healthy adults with a positive body image and a shame-free sex life. This is difficult to achieve if sex talks are avoided or if we are offended or frightened by our kid's questions, experiences, or normal development.

Society will tell our kids how to look and feel about sex, and it's rarely healthy or helpful. Not only is the focus about comparing and competing, but it's also about consumerism and buying whatever is suggested to be or look more like someone who is considered "sexy." And that's not to mention the explosion of the porn industry and the fact that boys and girls, often as young as ten years old, look to porn as a tutorial. This is a bottomless pit that takes our kids further from their true selves and keeps them more at the mercy of an unattainable, unsatisfying, and, too often, unsafe goal.

The advice given to kids and teens who are molested or assaulted is to tell a trusted adult, and the probability of them doing this is increased if parents have already discussed the difference between wanted and unwanted touch. Too many kids and teens I have worked with say they feel too guilty or embarrassed to share their abuse with their parents, usually because their parents have already demonstrated so much silence and discomfort when it comes to sex and sexual topics.

Kids can be given a direct and early message that unwanted or forced touch by an adult or peer is not okay and that they are never at fault. Kids can be given a direct and early message that you will always listen and help if they are afraid or confused and that together you will handle every conversation, no matter how difficult.

According to a 2017 study, "Parents are the single largest influence on their adolescents' decisions about sex, and parents underestimate the impact they have on their decisions."[16] This means that, like everything else in this book, parents need to focus on their own shame and challenges when it comes to sex so we don't pass along pain or trauma that doesn't belong to our children. As we free ourselves from believing that sex or sexuality is inappropriate or something to hide, we'll find it easier to talk to our kids and be open and responsive to their questions.

## Understanding Sexuality and Gender

*We are not what other people say we are. We are who
we know ourselves to be, and we are what we love.*

—LAVERNE COX, *actress and LGBTQ activist,
interviewed by Kelli Korducki,* Rookie *magazine*

As a parent it's critical to understand the difference between
**sexuality** (*who we are attracted to*) and **gender** (*a personal sense
of being a man or a woman or outside that gender binary*) and
to respect that every person has their own identification
when it comes to who they love and how they present.

Allowing your children to tell you who they are rather
than dictating what is expected gives them the freedom
to appreciate and respect who they are. Society is already
shouting gender-specific norms and expectations about
how boys and girls are supposed to look, speak, dress, and
act, but as parents we can buffer this system by allowing
our children to be themselves and advocate for their inherent expression, whatever it may be.

**Sex** can mean the act of sex and also *a person's bio-
logical makeup, their body and chromosomes, defined usually
as either "male" or "female" and including indeterminate sex*
(from the Human Rights Campaign), just as **sexuality** can
mean sexual activity but also *a person's sexual orientation or
preference.*

**Gender** is defined as *the social and cultural construction
of what it means to be a man or a woman, including roles, expectations, and behavior.* **Gender identity** is defined as *a person's*

*internal, deeply felt sense of being male or female (or something other or in between)*, and **gender expression** is *how someone expresses their sense of masculinity or femininity, or both, externally.*

**LGBTQ+** is shorthand for lesbian, gay, bisexual, transgender, and queer (or questioning). *LGB* refers to sexual orientation, and *T* refers to transgender or nonbinary identification, where gender identity or gender expression does not conform to the sex that was assigned at birth. *Queer* is used to demonstrate a contrast from mainstream, heteronormative society, an umbrella term that can be used by anyone in the LGBTQ+ community. It can convey both orientation and a sense of community.

There is vast diversity in the LGBTQ+ community, and the common lists of terminology are rarely comprehensive, so the + sign is used to indicate its evolving nature. Identification is a living language that's not limited to five letters, and our work as parents and allies is to listen and learn so we can respect each person's story and how they identify.

When it comes to gender identification, appropriate pronouns and figuring out if someone identifies as he/him, she/her, or they/them demonstrates dignity and understanding. In early prepandemic 2020, we hosted a transgender/nonbinary panel at our Zen Parenting Conference, and all of the participants, adults and teens, said they preferred to be asked their pronouns and appreciated it when others shared theirs in turn. This expectation has also been shared by my clients who are raising transgender children. The practice of sharing pronouns makes it easier for people to introduce themselves (in person or electronically through email signature) and have a common understanding before a conversation or relationship begins.

Again, gender identity is different from sexual orientation. Sexual orientation is about *who someone is attracted to,* and gender identity is about *a personal sense of being a man or a woman or outside that gender binary.* Transgender people can be gay, lesbian, bisexual, or straight.

This leads to an understanding of **intersectionality**, a term coined in 1989 by Professor Kimberlé Crenshaw to describe how race, class, gender, and other individual characteristics "intersect" with one another and overlap. Intersectionality is best explained by understanding that it takes into account *all of who a person is, all of the factors of identification*—including race, indigeneity, socioeconomic status, gender, gender identity, sexual orientation, age, (dis)ability, spirituality, immigration/refugee status, language, and education—specifically focusing on how this impacts individual experiences, as well as the collective work we need to do to uproot inequality and injustice.

When I talk to parents about sex, gender, or anything that feels different or expansive, there is initially a lot of defensiveness or complaints that it's too much to understand or that things should be simpler. While the desire for simplicity is understandable, it's simply not possible when talking about complex human beings. It was "simpler" when we were growing up because the safety and space to share weren't available, not because differences didn't exist.

Walt Whitman wrote, *"I am large, I contain multitudes,"* pointing to the fact that human beings have paradoxical aspects that require specificity and understanding.[17] People thrive and develop a foundational confidence if they are seen and heard, and we love our children well by supporting them as they express the many aspects of their unique selves. It's our job to do the ongoing, necessary work to become more educated and aware so we can continue to show up as competent allies for our children and the entire LGBTQ+ community.

## Disrupting Gender Stereotypes and Norms

The problem with gender is that it prescribes how we should be rather than recognizing how we are. Imagine how much happier we would be, how much freer to be our true individual selves, if we didn't have the weight of gender expectations.

—CHIMAMANDA NGOZI ADICHIE,
We Should All Be Feminists

As an advocate and therapist for women and girls my whole professional career, married to a man who coaches men and runs a national men's group, we live and breathe this conversation. As we raise our three daughters, we constantly confront our own gendered experiences, forcing us to speak up or take the time to listen. Our work exposes us to the vastly differing experiences of men and women and how as parents we have conscious, and unconscious, gender-specific expectations of sons and daughters. The challenges and discrepancies live deep inside of us and our culture, and all genders end up suffering the consequences.

This conversation needs to be first informed by the fact that gender issues become even more complex for those in the LGBTQ+ community, specifically when it comes to nonbinary or trans identity. And women of color are further disadvantaged, leading to "linked forms of injustice that are not captured in mainstream research."[18] With that understanding, I'll speak to the general aspects of gender issues, with the understanding that intersectionality exacerbates and compounds these inequalities.

A lot of women, me being one of them, were raised by parents who told us we could do anything, and while there is absolute truth in this optimism, girls inevitably confront a number of cultural and societal roadblocks. Research shows that by the age of six, girls believe they are less likely than boys to be "really, really smart," profoundly influencing academic and career choices long after. And while most parents don't consciously endorse this stereotype, a 2014 report found that American parents Googled "Is my son a genius?" more than twice as often as they Googled "Is my daughter a genius?"[19]

We live in a patriarchy where only 19 heads of state out of a possible 196 are women, and men dominate the highest-paying fields. Gender pay gaps are present in every industry and profession, and only 55 of the 500 richest people in the world are women. Women's education lags behind men's, and most women around the world aren't compensated for the work they do to benefit the economy, from child care and elderly caregiving to home management. More than a third of women worldwide have experienced physical or sexual violence at some point in their lives, and female genital mutilation, femicide, gender-based violence, and early marriage are still part of life for billions of girls and women.

Women used to make up the majority in the workforce, but since the pandemic nearly half of the more than 2.3 million women who make up the workforce have left, with Black mothers reportedly leaving the workforce at more than twice the rate of white mothers. Studies also found that during the pandemic working moms suffered from disproportionate levels of burnout and stress, with mothers having to decide between child care and work and feeling more of the weight when it came to decision making regarding school and health-care concerns.[20]

The fact that parents are Googling "Is my daughter overweight?" about 70 percent more often than "Is my son overweight?" demonstrates a cultural focus and paradox around a girl's appearance. In Mary Pipher's acclaimed book *Reviving Ophelia*, she says, "Girls struggle with mixed messages: Be beautiful, but beauty is only skin deep. Be sexy, but not sexual. Be honest, but don't hurt anyone's feelings. Be independent, but be nice. Be smart, but not so smart you threaten boys."[21]

When Rachel Simmons, author of *Enough As She Is*, spoke at our Zen Parenting Conference, she asked girls to sit the way a typical guy sits and then asked guys to sit the way a typical girl sits. The girls spread out and relaxed, and the men pulled themselves up and got smaller—a demonstration that guys have learned or inherited permission to take up space in every sense of the word, while women understand they are supposed to stay small and nice. As Soraya Chemaly says in *Rage Becomes Her: The Power of Women's Anger*, "We are so busy teaching girls to be likeable that we often forget to teach them, as we do boys, that they should be respected."[22]

The majority of women who show up in my office are between thirty-five and fifty-five, and they are experiencing what feels like a midlife crisis. Through marriage, parenthood, or work, they are realizing that they can't and don't want to hold on to the facade that they developed in childhood and as a young adult. They describe feeling like they are falling apart, which is actually an accurate description, because what they pieced together in their early lives is beginning to chip away. Their true selves are doing everything they can to emerge, through discomfort like anxiety, depression, physical ailments, or dissatisfaction in marriage or parenthood. The pain is their gateway, a deeply uncomfortable journey that is necessary for their future well-being.

Most women have become highly aware of the invisible labor of their lives, how they are expected to be striving working women while not missing a beat as a doting wife, parent, friend, daughter, and homemaker. They also feel pressure to stay young and look beautiful, spending a lot of money on products or clothes that make them attractive to others. A lot of energy is put into working out or eating healthy, and my clients who don't do this feel horrible about themselves, believing they are endlessly dropping the ball on their health and appearance.

Women and men fall so easily into stereotypical roles, and the same-sex couples I work with have reported similar experiences, with one partner taking on the more traditionally feminine or caretaker role, while the other works and is less involved in the home. As Gemma Hartley says in her book *Fed Up*, "While women have spent the past few decades being encouraged to reach for the masculine ideal of success, being told they can become anything their hearts desire in the professional realm, they have not been relieved of any of the invisible labor that waits for them when they return home."[23]

Invisible labor, as Hartley defines it, is "emotion management and life management combined. It is the unpaid, invisible work we do to keep those around us comfortable and happy." In the past twenty years, every woman I have worked with has described feeling the weight of invisible labor in one form or another, with one client describing it as "tabs" that are open in her head at all times: coordinating doctors appointments, Amazon returns, grocery store runs and meal preparation, vacations, gifts and plans for holidays, staying in touch with extended family, house cleaning and maintenance, managing the children's emotions and behavior, and paying attention to schoolwork and extracurricular activities,

while contemplating or worrying about any possible un-
met needs. It's a continuation of a deeply ingrained belief
that women must uphold the expectations of past motherhood, while also maintaining the expectations of present-
day womanhood.

The pandemic was especially hard on women,
ratcheting up all the existing tensions and adding new
anxiety-provoking layers. Millions of women were already
supporting themselves and their families on insufficient
wages, and the lockdowns increased unemployment and
led to millions of jobs disappearing. Working mothers
were already shouldering the majority of family caregiving responsibilities within a child-care system that was
insufficient even before the pandemic. The disruptions to
day-care centers, schools, and after-school programs were
hard on everyone, but it was typically working mothers
who picked up the extra responsibilities and were more
frequently reducing their hours or leaving their jobs entirely to make everything work.[24]

My clients talk to me about the incessant nature of invisible labor and, if they have a career outside the home,
how they are paid less for doing the same work as men
(and women of color are paid less than white women).
They share how as the "daughter" in their family of origin,
they are expected to care for their aging parents and are
sometimes even expected to care for the parents of their
partners. They talk about the impact of their experiences
with sexual harassment, assault, and other types of sexual
trauma and grieve how young they were when they began

to be sexualized. They share how much they hate their bodies, how they continue to struggle with decades-long eating disorders, and how they aren't interested in sex because they feel completely disconnected from what they want or need.

Some feel saddened by their lack of strong friendships and the fact that they don't trust other women because they were taught to believe that women were untrustworthy (which results in them believing they must be untrustworthy, too). They worry that if they stay home with their children, they are missing a career, and if they thrive in their career, they are missing parenthood. Regardless of their issues, the common theme is that they feel they are doing it wrong, toggling between the two voices that Brené Brown's research demonstrates are born out of shame: *Not good enough* and *Who do you think you are?* [25]

I support women in questioning their behavior and speaking up for what they need, but these two voices ring just as loudly in my ears. *Not good enough* and *Who do you think you are?* are the extremes of our programming that tend to distract or paralyze us. Early motherhood woke me up to these voices and my deep-rooted beliefs about gender expectations. I recognized how I had built my career and put myself through grad school, which eventually led to a therapist position at one of the top hospitals in Chicago. When I had my first daughter, I felt like the family-restructuring expectation fell to me, so I left my job. As the mother, I felt I was doing what was expected, that I needed to find a new life-work balance without even investigating or discussing what could, or would, change for my husband.

One day, about six months after my daughter was born, I realized that when I left the house, I either took my daughter with me or did what felt like "asking permission" for my husband to watch her. I would see my husband come and go as he pleased; his lifestyle and decision making hadn't changed much at all, but I had limited freedom and was tasked with asking for help. We now refer to this experience as the "Target story" because it was our first big argument about the differences between our expectations as parents. I remember saying over and over again, "Why do I have to *ask* to go to Target, and you *go* to Target whenever you want?"

The Target story became the metaphor for work, life, body changes, pressure, decision making, and expectations—I could have just as easily said, "Why has my life changed completely in every possible way, but you are still doing all the same things?" This cracked open a conversation that continues to this day: What are the messages and programming that created this inequality when it comes to parenting? How did we so easily fall into these gender-specific patterns when prior to having children we felt like equals?

While men and women today tend to report that their decisions are mutual and in alignment with more egalitarian ideals, the outcomes still lean more toward the father maintaining his goals while the mother alters or sacrifices her expectations.[26] Author Brigid Schulte addresses this in her book *Overwhelmed: Work, Love, and Play When No One Has the Time*: "Grousing about how little husbands do at home is a regular and tiresomely predictable social exchange. And though the sociologist Arlie Hochschild first wrote in the 1980s about how women come home from a full day of work to a 'second shift' of housework and childcare, the same is true in the 21st century. Even though time studies show men are doing more around the house and with the kids, women are still doing twice as much. Sociologists call it the 'stalled gender revolution.'"[27]

This is indicative of a deep belief system that we learn early, a belief system that can show up unexpectedly as women make bigger decisions, like running for office, starting a business, accepting praise or acknowledgment, or trusting women to lead our country. The dismantling of "niceness" and questioning the societal ideals of what it means to be female necessitate a deep interrogation of ourselves and the systems that benefit from our early training.

These systems are oppressive and limiting to women and also harmful to boys and men. Early on boys are taught such a narrow view of what it means to be masculine, forcing them to live inside what Tony Porter, chief executive officer (CEO) of A Call to Men, calls "the man box," a basic understanding of how men are collectively socialized. Beliefs inside the man box include (but are not limited to): women are weak, while men don't express feelings and emotions (except anger), must be athletic and courageous, must show no fear, must have no pain, and don't ask for help.

So much of this runs opposite to female societal expectations, meaning manhood gets defined by the ability to distance themselves from the female experience. Done effectively, it creates a lack of interest in what women need or what it means to be a woman, except when it comes to sexual conquests. Teaching men to value women less and view them as property or objects also leads to the objectification and violence against women and girls.

Former National Football League player Joe Ehrmann, now president of the InSideOut Initiative, focuses on what he calls the three lies of masculinity—athletic ability, sexual conquest, and economic success—and how men suffer the consequences of believing that these are the only things that make them worthy. He says in the documentary *The Mask You Live In,* "The three most destructive words that every man receives when he's a boy is when he's told to 'be a man.'"[28]

Research shows that compared to girls, boys in the United States are more likely to be diagnosed with a behavior disorder, prescribed stimulant medications, fail out of school, binge drink, commit a violent crime, take their own lives, or some combination thereof. A study authored by Dr. Robert Blum at Johns Hopkins looked at the development of gender stereotypes in early adolescence and found that boys were more likely than girls to report adversity such as physical neglect, sexual abuse, and violence victimization and that boys were eleven times more likely to be engaged in violence, compared to four times among girls. When Blum conducted his study in 2017, the only group that had experienced decreased life expectancy was men over fifty, mainly due to self-directed violence and access to guns.[29]

Loneliness isn't inherently gendered, but men in particular tend to struggle with expressing deep feelings or forming meaningful connections, finding it easier to talk about football or politics than to admit to their pain or life challenges. This experience is what propelled my husband and his friend Frank to cofound MenLiving, a nationwide organization that focuses on men engaging in authentic conversations through social activities and community engagement.

Todd knew something needed to change when he realized that, after spending a full weekend with his guy friends, he had nothing to report when I asked how each of them was doing. In contrast, I would spend thirty minutes with a girlfriend and catch up on all the important issues of her life. He recognized how his conversations with men rarely went below the surface, and although he was spending time with friends, he was constantly missing opportunities to support or feel supported. The guys who participate in MenLiving are the same guys who watch football games at the bar and show up to watch their kids' soccer games, but instead of having to put on a facade or avoid anything personal, they can safely invest in honest and supportive conversations and learning.

Self-awareness for both women and men contributes to the pursuit of gender equality, with tangible benefits for everyone involved.[30] On a purely economic basis, having greater economic opportunities for women creates greater prosperity for all. More women in power means better democratic outcomes for everyone, and equal pay and opportunity lead to better workplace cultures. Gender diversity in business leadership leads to more creative decision making, greater returns for organizations, and more sustainable outcomes for the economy. Treating both men's and women's ideas with equal respect increases our chance of building a global society that avoids ecological damage and works for everyone.

## Valuing Mental Wellness

> Anything that's human is mentionable, and anything that is mentionable can be more manageable. When we can talk about our feelings, they become less overwhelming, less upsetting, and less scary.
>
> —FRED ROGERS

Mental wellness begins with the awareness of and allowance for emotions, a willingness to understand and identify the many ways that our kids feel.

This means that telling our children that some feelings are unacceptable or punishing them for having certain feelings will lead to an inevitable internal conflict. Making them feel guilty or ashamed of their emotions can lead to them abandoning parts of themselves or believing there is something inherently wrong with them.

If children express difficult feelings and are met with reminders of why they shouldn't feel that way or that they should just "feel happy," they learn that difficult emotional states are not welcome or understood, leading them to believe that struggling isn't acceptable or manageable.

All emotional states, including disappointment, failure, grief, and loss, need to be recognized and processed, starting when they are very young. As parents we can discuss these normal aspects of being a human and share our own journey when it comes to pain and resilience. Role modeling plays a significant role when it comes to mental well-being. If parents or family members never discuss their own pain or processes, kids are left to feel as if their pain is unique or wrong, making it more difficult to share or ask for help.

Parents should never burden their children with their own pain or expect that it's a child's responsibility to take care of them (in clinical speak, this is called *parentification*, where a child is expected to act as a parent to the adults and other children), but parents can normalize their own experience with typical emotions, demonstrating to the child that all feelings are a shared human experience.

Similar to sexuality, shame plays a big role in kids' and teens' unwillingness to share their most difficult feelings and thoughts. When I work with young girls, teens, or even college students, we talk about the "voice in the head," the one that tells them they aren't enough or are inherently wrong or not good enough. I remind them that all humans have this voice, no matter their age, and while it always seems to have an opinion, it lies and doesn't deserve our absorbed attention.

Just acknowledging this voice offers young people a collective sigh of relief and an understanding that something they fear or worry about is actually quite common. This opens the door to other conversations about how their brain works, and when my children or students are open to the conversation, I can really go off about the absolute coolness of interpersonal neurobiology. The bottom line is that all of us experience dark and scary thoughts, and this doesn't make us bad people; it makes us human.

Talking to children about mental health from a young age can help them relate to their feelings, allowing them to become more resilient and decrease the stigma around mental health. Tools for mental well-being are just as important as learning about physical health, yet so many of us put it off indefinitely, not wanting to "expose" our kids to things like depression or anxiety.

Yet the National Institute of Mental Health reports that about 3.2 million twelve- to seventeen-year-olds have had at least one major depressive episode within the past twelve months, and according to the National Institutes of Health, nearly 1 in 3 of all adolescents ages thirteen to eighteen will experience an anxiety disorder.[31] Suicide is the second-leading cause of death for people ages ten to thirty-four, and the most concerning part of all of these statistics is that they were true before the pandemic even began.[32]

Letting your kids know that they can talk to you or any other trusted adult about their feelings allows them to share what hurts rather than working so hard to repress or deny. Your kids need to know that professional help is always available, whether it be the social worker at school or finding an individual therapist. As a parent, I often tell my kids that while they can always talk to me, talking to other trusted adults or seeking outside professional help is always an option. They know all about my own experiences with therapy and coaching, and when they ask I share the tools and tips that have been most helpful to my own mental well-being.

Normalizing the need for support in difficult times empowers children to ask for help when they are hurting. Too many kids believe that whatever they are experiencing is hopeless, but once they begin to share, not only do they experience the relief of speaking their pain, but they also realize the common humanity of their hurt and struggle, gaining greater access to the many supportive options (therapeutic, medicinal, nutritional, and educational, just to name a few) that are always available.

With my own kids and younger clients, I use the latest celebrity and pop culture stories to discuss mental wellness. Whether it be someone who died by suicide, someone checking into rehab, or someone who is openly sharing their own diagnosis or treatment, it's an opportunity to discuss how all of us experience pain, regardless of money or status. These discussions also begin after witnessing the story of a movie or television character and through the discussion of song lyrics and how they help us feel or relate.

During the pandemic and at the height of the racial justice protests, emotions were heightened beyond what we thought we could endure. To deal with so much change and uncertainty, rest and self-care needed to become priorities, not a consumer type of self-care where we just took care of how we looked, but a deep, internal kind of self-care where processing fear and difficult emotions became essential for daily living.

So much of life came to a grinding halt, which was difficult and destabilizing, but it also offered us the time to focus on what really mattered: connection with loved ones, a slower pace, taking care of each other, and using art, movement, singing, and collaborating to speak to the shared pain we were experiencing. These realizations weren't new ideas; they were what has always been necessary but too easily forgotten.

In Glennon Doyle's book *Carry on, Warrior,* she explains that the Greek root of the word *crisis* is "to sift," meaning to shake out what's unneeded and keep what's most important.[33] Our cumulative crises in 2020 pointed to what's most important, and if we are smart we will move forward without forgetting what we learned. What "sifts" through during crisis creates space for what's most important, offering us more opportunity to make our mental wellness a priority.

# USING THE CHAKRA SYSTEM

*To Better Understand Ourselves,*
*Our Kids, Our World*

Until you make the unconscious conscious,
it will direct your life and you will call it fate.

—CARL JUNG

## Why Chakras?

Few of us have the measure of self-awareness that we think we do. This means that the majority of us are moving through each day on autopilot, allowing our subconscious mind to rule our lives. And while our subconscious minds are incredibly powerful as they build and rebuild our bodies and keep trillions of complex life-sustaining processes working properly, this mysterious driving force also needs conscious suggestions to achieve our desired outcomes as partners, parents, and healthy members of society.

This means we need to take inventory of our histories and current ways of being, and we need to become introspective about how we feel and what we do. As a clinician trained in a medical/Western model who studies and practices mindfulness, yoga, and more Eastern concepts, I've found that one of the most effective ways to bring these pieces together is through the study and understanding of the chakra system.

Chakras are the concentrated energy centers of the body, seven along the spine, through the neck and the crown of your head. *Chakra* is a Sanskrit term meaning "wheel" or "disk," and chakras are responsible for taking in, incorporating, and emanating energy to keep us functioning in a healthy and productive way.

Chakras play a key role in Ayurvedic medicine and yoga, and if you've experienced body work such as Reiki or acupuncture, you've experienced the release of energy blockages or restored balance through the workings of the chakra system.

Understanding chakras is a never-ending education; the system is complex and in-depth, and there are plenty of texts and teachers that are solely dedicated to understanding them in their entirety. This book shares just the basic elements of the chakra system as a tool to practice self-awareness and begin the process of unlearning to rediscover ourselves.

Those who want to know more about chakras should search beyond this text to study its intricacy and healing possibilities, and those who don't feel connected to chakras can simply view this as a framework or metaphor for human existence, a way to discuss the individual aspects of yourself and your parenting.

Each one of the chakras reflects a basic, inalienable right. Not trusting or practicing the right can lead to a "blockage"; reclaiming the right contributes to healing and self-understanding. The rights, in order from one to seven, are: *the right to be, the right to feel, the right to act, the right to love and be loved, the right to speak and hear truth, the right to see, and the right to know.*

Practicing our birthrights keeps our energy healthy and leads to the development of our emotional intelligence, or EQ. In his book *Emotional Intelligence,* Daniel Goleman explains that self-awareness, self-regulation, self-motivation, and empathy are the keys to physical and mental well-being. There is also an ethical dimension: as we go through life, the sense that we are on course with our values becomes an inner rudder, the basis of our choices and the defining of our integrity.

The chakras are vertically aligned, running from the sacrum to the top of the head, and at each stage we gain a more refined self-understanding and greater access to personal power. Chakras are interconnected and affect one another, but each chakra carries out a specific function. The process of researching and understanding each chakra energy is reminiscent of the hero's journey, a mastering of skills on the path to reclaiming our lives and sharing what we know with our children.

## Set an Intention

Before we begin any type of self-awareness journey, it's important to have some clarity about what we want to learn and why. We don't need to have unwavering answers to these questions, because if the journey is interesting, these initial intentions will expand and evolve. But if we are seeking new horizons, it's important to at least have a sense of where we want to go.

The focus can be finding something new (more peace, more time for myself) or something we want to practice (practice self-compassion, practice being kinder to loved ones). These initial intentions can set the stage for what you learn along the way. Again, they will most likely expand, evolve, or change altogether: going on a self-awareness journey is inherently unpredictable. But it can be the grounding element that kicks off your experience and maybe offers a sense of excitement about what you might discover along the way.

Talking with a therapist, coach, or group about your deepening sense of awareness is beneficial and may help you in putting what you learn into practice. Change comes not just from navel gazing, but from our ability to practice what we know with others. We learn about ourselves and then apply our learning to our relationships and interactions with the world.

My clients love to talk about their self-awareness, delving into a deep understanding of their histories and why they do what they do, but they often have difficulty putting what they learn into meaningful practice. They continue to make the same mistakes, expecting different outcomes because their intellectual understanding has shifted. Again, Zen Parenting is going beyond intellectual understanding and investing in the *practice* of what you know. You can continually explain yourself to others, but until you take responsibility and change your actions, things will remain the same.

Changing our actions can feel awkward and vulnerable, and we may question the process or find discomfort in the practice. When I started communicating in a more honest way, I found that I initially came on too harsh, like a faucet turned on full blast. I had to work on modulating my emotions and expression, and like any new thing, it took time and humility. This is again why self-awareness and connection to others are practices, because they are about present-moment awareness and responsiveness rather than a set of rules that we follow perfectly.

I have worked with many academic teachers, body workers, yoga instructors, therapists, and coaches along the way, and while all the experiences were enlightening, they were not all positive. Several of my teachers became more interested in my following their lead than in my finding my own way. The relationship would usually begin with vital learning and connection, but then devolve into a hierarchal relationship where I was expected to follow without question rather than question and grow.

It felt similar to an authoritarian parenting relationship, where a parent imparts information and expects the child to mimic back as directed, but as educator Jean Piaget recognized, children are not "empty vessels to be filled with knowledge"; they are "active builders of knowledge—little scientists who construct their own theories of the world."[1]

This is true of both children and adults. Be wary of anyone who tells you there is one way or that you must blindly follow for any type of understanding. Every person has the right to trust their own internal knowing as they learn from others. We all have a unique inner voice that will guide us along the way, and while we are relational beings who need support from others, the hopeful outcome is that we learn to trust ourselves and what we know, that we befriend ourselves and have faith in what we have to offer.

Learning to trust ourselves while learning from others is a delicate balance that the best teachers do their best to offer. This has probably been the hardest part of my journey, because while I found many people who taught me to trust myself, several played on old wounds that reaffirmed I was untrustworthy or required their specific guidance. Moving in and out of these patterns was painful, like reliving childhood trauma, but they are also the experiences that contributed the most to the way I teach and write today.

What's discussed in this book and on the *Zen Parenting Radio* podcast are things you most likely know but have lost touch with somewhere along the way. When you find resonance, which means *a common vibration of two things moving in unison,* in something being written or spoken, please understand that what you just "learned" was already yours, that words are hitting you on an internal level that makes you feel seen. As a student, this is my favorite feeling, and as a teacher, it's my favorite offering. We are all sharing universal experiences and principles that, when heard at the right time, can wake us up to ourselves.

This means that I or any other teacher can see, support, and offer what we know, but we do not know more than you about you; everyone must develop their own practice and sense of personal understanding. If something resonates, it's an opportunity to go out and learn more, to ask questions and ask for help whenever you need it. Our friend and teacher the Reverend Ed Bacon once said that we should each be president of our own lives, that we should all have a cabinet of people we trust to call on for support and guidance, but in the end our final decision should always belong to us. This book or any book suggested may be part of your cabinet, but allow them to guide you closer to self-trust rather than to something or somebody else that claims to have all the answers.

This understanding should also inform your parenting, allowing you to recognize that you are an essential member of your child's cabinet, but they are still the president of their lives. You are there to guide and inform, to build connection and offer input—and then you also need to let go, trusting that they will find their own way. Children will not always choose perfectly, and they will make mistakes because their growth depends on both challenge and resilience, pain and joy. They need to know you are there to help them, without feeling as if they owe you or need to find a way around you—or that, at worst, they can't trust you.

Better to offer them a wealth of information rather than a single point of view. It comes back to questioning whether we trust who our kids can become. If we have done our own work and experienced our own inner knowing and voice, it's easier to recognize that our kids have the same voice. They are resilient like we are; they have a knowing like we do. From this place we can give ourselves fully and then set them free, with the roots and wings they require to live a life of meaning.

But if we have not done our own work or do not trust who we are, we may unconsciously parent from a place of fear and distrust, altering how our children see us and themselves. Our greatest gift to our children is to do our own work so we can accurately see them and offer them guidance from a grounded place. This is an ongoing work in progress, but we can begin by revisiting our own inalienable rights, starting from the ground up.

A right to **know**                                CROWN
A right to **see**                            THIRD EYE
A right to **speak
and hear truth**                              THROAT
A right to **love
and be loved**                                 HEART
A right to **act**                    SOLAR PLEXUS
A right to **feel**                          SACRAL
A right to **be**                              ROOT

## Chakra One

# THE RIGHT TO BE

*Establishing Our Foundation*

Base of the spine, sacrum

**RED**

A tree lives on its roots. If you change the root, you
change the tree. Culture lives in human beings. If you
change the human heart the culture will follow.

—**JANE HIRSHFIELD,** *"A Larger Yes: Poetry as a Vessel of
Discovery, Mindfulness, Expansion and Engagement"*

### Body Foundation

The first chakra, or root chakra, is our foundation. It's our
base and anchor, establishing a sense of safety and feelings of belonging. Uncertain and scary experiences from
everyday challenges to a global pandemic shake the foundation of our lives and throw our sense of safety out of balance. Uncertainty uproots us, untethering us from what

we thought we knew. But no matter the situation, we can shift to focusing on replanting and discovering new ways to ground ourselves even in the midst of change.

Uncertainty forces us to reconsider our grounding forces and where we have been placing importance. We may have been focused on what we have and what we do and then come to realize that this is not solid ground. In the midst of challenge, things and titles may be taken away or not offer the solace or connection we need. This is an opportunity to go deeper, to get back to our original roots and deeper sense of knowing.

Understanding our foundation, our root chakra, is the beginning of our journey. In the body, it's located at the base of the spine called the sacrum, with the legs acting as roots, pushing downward from the base of the spine. Understanding the foundation of our bodies establishes the connection to ourselves and our lives. Throughout our lives we are repetitiously taught that the mind is superior to the body, leading us to believe that our mind should be in control of the body. This undermines the natural intelligence of the body, distracting us from the signals and signs that are there to help us.

Body disconnection is a cultural epidemic, leaving us detached from ourselves and our own inner knowing. Not only did I experience this myself, but it tends to be a consistent theme with my female clients. They spend a great deal of time talking about their own body disconnection, how they feel uncomfortable in their skin and unable to get in touch with what they feel and why. Geneen Roth, author of *Women, Food, and God,* explains, "People feel discomfort verging on self-loathing about their bodies. They don't really own or live in these bodies. They're not feeling what it's like to be inside their body, they have no awareness of what that's like. Most people live in our minds. We think we are our minds."[1]

**Feeling disconnected from our bodies disassociates us from our actions, leading us to consciously or unconsciously hurt ourselves.** We may do it through overeating or drinking, smoking or vaping, or cutting, as so many young girls tend to do. Self-harm distracts us from our minds so we can find some kind of control, release emotional tension, or feel something when we feel numb. We stop paying attention or even noticing signals of pain and override messages of fear or discomfort to avoid acting on what our bodies are trying to tell us. We forget that we live inside the body we are ignoring or harming, losing track of the fact that our bodies have the wisdom to keep us alive and well. Establishing a foundation begins with bringing mind and body back together; it's not about choosing one or the other but about joining what was never supposed to be separated.

While Western culture has historically focused on *dualism,* a model articulated by René Descartes that the mind and body are totally independent of each other, research has demonstrated that *monism,* an understanding that mind and body are not separate, is more medically sound and effective. This view has been held by Eastern, Native American, and other indigenous cultures, and Western training and treatment methods are now catching up.

We know that stress and tension can cause headaches and stomach problems and even lead to high blood pressure. We accept that chronic health problems can affect emotions, resulting in depression and anxiety. We utilize the research-based effectiveness of group therapy during cancer treatments and practice yoga not only for body flexibility but to deal with stress and anxiety as well.

What's going on in our body impacts our mind and emotions and vice versa, which is why body disconnection threatens overall well-being. Bessel van der Kolk, author of *The Body Keeps the Score: Brain, Mind, and Body in the Healing of Trauma*, explores "the extreme disconnection from the body that so many people with histories of trauma and neglect experience" and all the paths to recovery.[2]

He focuses on agency, or what scientists call *interoception*, our awareness of body-based feelings such as a growling stomach, dry mouth, tense muscles, or a racing heart. Awareness of these sensations enables us to experience emotions such as hunger, fullness, pain, relaxation, anxiety, and safety. At the most basic level, interoception allows us to answer the question *How do I feel?* and knowing *what* we feel is the first step to knowing *why* we feel that way. If we are aware of what our body feels and we have some insight into why it's reacting this way, we can manage it. If we can't feel it, we can't self-regulate what we don't understand.

If we experienced any kind of trauma in our lives (and to a certain degree, most of us have), it disrupts our ability to know what we feel and whether we should trust gut feelings. This lack of self-trust causes us to believe we are threatened when we aren't, leading to an antagonistic relationship with our own bodies.

Our past pain and trauma can make us feel unsafe inside our bodies, even leading to an overriding sense of inner discomfort, like chronic anxiety or depression. Feeling overwhelmed by constant visceral warning signs can lead us to ignore or distrust feelings until we are literally hiding from ourselves. The more the internal signs are pushed away, the more likely they will take over (*what we resist persists*), leading us to shut off completely or become intensely panicked, leading to a fear of fear itself.

To regain our sense of agency, we have to practice befriending our bodies and feeling what we feel. Van der Kolk explains, "Trauma victims cannot recover until they become familiar with and befriend the sensations in their bodies. Being frightened means that you live in a body that is always on guard. . . . Physical self-awareness is the first step in releasing the tyranny of the past."[3]

The paradox of healing is that connection can feel vulnerable or terrifying, but social support and a sense of community are the foundations on which we rebuild a healthy sense of self. What normalizes and repairs our ability to read danger and safety correctly is human connection. It's not just being in the presence of others, but being truly heard by the people around us, a feeling that we are seen and understood.

It's vital for adults to reflect on their own childhoods and work through any trauma, ideally with a professional. This is an opportunity to become a more integrated self, bringing mind and body back together, and also an opportunity to consider how to best raise our own children. Inability to at least consider our own traumatic experiences can lead to our repeating toxic patterns from our childhood and leave us unable to role model mind-body connection for our own children.

The latest research tells us that adverse childhood experiences, or ACEs, between the ages of zero and seventeen have lasting negative effects on health and overall well-being. Children growing up with toxic stress tend to have more difficulty maintaining healthy and stable relationships. Unprocessed traumatic experiences from childhood can increase the risks of injury, sexually transmitted infections, teen pregnancy, and a wide range of chronic diseases and leading causes of death such as cancer, diabetes, heart disease, and suicide. Many children end up facing even greater exposure to toxic stress due to historical and ongoing traumas from systemic racism and poverty, including limited educational and economic opportunities.[4]

Previous generations did not put much focus on seeing and hearing a child, and there are still modern parents practicing the fifteenth-century English proverb *Children should be seen and not heard*. But children develop a sense of self when they are seen and heard and when they have opportunity to process painful and traumatic experiences with someone who listens and understands. This kind of validation helps them accept their emotional experiences as real and meaningful, leading to self-compassion and the capacity to be empathic with others.

But to hear and validate children, we first need to hear and validate ourselves. We need to reconcile our histories and find safety in our bodies so we aren't misperceiving our surroundings and constantly recycling old pain. We need to pay attention to our own needs so we can role model the importance of self-awareness and self-care and why the mind-body connection will lead to the best possible life outcomes.

## Root to Rise

In yoga we often say "root to rise," which means we need a well-intentioned foundation if we want to stretch and move safely and effectively. In the physical practice we ground our feet and legs before growing and extending. Off the yoga mat, we can mentally and emotionally ground ourselves before moving forward and making decisions.

Rooting is about being mindful before making choices, about taking a breath and getting centered before acting. Before you say something to your partner or your kids, connect with your strong foundation, even put your feet on the floor to feel it, and decide if what you are about to say is essential.

One practice is that before you speak, consider the acronym T-H-I-N-K:

> T—Is it true?
> H—Is it helpful?
> I—Is it inspiring?
> N—Is it necessary?
> K—Is it kind?

If not, maybe what you have to say isn't essential. Taking the time to even consider *one* of these letters may keep you from impulsively reacting. Connecting with the root chakra slows the mind and body, allowing for calmer and more thoughtful responses.

The root chakra is like a well-planted tree, with an understanding that trees do not just grow up and out; they also grow down and into. Similar to when a bird gets ready to fly, it hunkers down and centers itself, or when a swimmer prepares to dive or a basketball player bends the knees to shoot, they are rooting themselves before the rise.

The root chakra reminds us to live with the natural rhythms of nature, to understand that if we don't establish a foundation, we could fall over or be at the mercy of the wind. It also offers us safer alignment physically and better intention emotionally. Paying attention to this chakra and consistently grounding ourselves allows our nervous system to calm so we can speak with clarity and confidence rather than fear.

## Physical and Emotional Safety

The root chakra keeps us grounded and roots us to familial beliefs that lead to our identity and sense of belonging. It's all about family dynamics and basic needs like feeling safe, supported, and provided for.

As a society, we are very focused on the physical safety of children. We take them to the doctor for checkups and vaccines; we get obsessed with proper nutrition, car seats, and helmets. We even use phone apps to track where our children are at all times. But we think less about their emotional safety, their ability to feel safe inside their own minds and bodies.

Their emotional well-being, their spirit, their "beingness" are just as vital for their health as their physicality. The Centers for Disease Control and Prevention have found that both anxiety and depression are on the rise for children of all ages, and it's been very apparent in my own clinical practice, especially during the pandemic.[5] While every child has their own story and situation, one way to lessen the burden that children carry is to be invested in and understanding about what's going on inside of them.

It's important to know that the daily interactions you have with your children impact their emotional well-being. Cognitive scientists at the Massachusetts Institute of Technology found that learning does not come from talking *at* children; it's about engaging them in a back-and-forth conversation. It's less about the words you use (content) and more about how you say things (context), supporting them through conversation and allowing them to offer their perspectives.[6]

It's also important to know that your words and messages become the running tape that lives inside your child's head. The helpful messages will serve them, but if the messages are consistently negative or cruel, these are the messages they will return to in adulthood, often leading to self-sabotaging behaviors or beliefs that change isn't possible. Parental interaction and communication develop the inner belief system, setting the stage for how children feel about themselves and what they believe about the world.

As Albert Einstein said, "The most important decision we make is whether we believe we live in a friendly or hostile universe."[7] The question is about examining our core positioning and baseline perception. If we can build a foundation of interacting with our kids in a way that demonstrates they are innately good and capable, that develops their sturdy foundation.

We can discuss and acknowledge darkness and also remind them that light is always available. We can accept and understand fear and also remind them that love is who we are. It's a dance of acknowledging shadow and light, that the highs and lows of life all exist in contrast with each other.

We wouldn't know joy if we've never been sad, and we wouldn't know safety if we've never been lost. This is how children develop a sense of emotional safety, of feeling rooted in the belief that what they feel is okay and that they are safe within themselves.

## Survival and Connection

As a parent, connection is being physically present and emotionally present, by engaging yourself in your child's experience and imagining what it's like to be them. It's about paying attention so your children feel like you "get" them, that you are doing all you can to attune to their experience. On the *Zen Parenting Radio* podcast, Todd and I always talk about removing our adult glasses so we can put on our kid glasses—meaning that we need to remember that kids are not little adults; they don't have a fully developed brain or lifetime of experience like we do.

We need to put ourselves in our kids' shoes and re-member how difficult it can be to share a toy, lose a friend, or have a first breakup. Putting on your kid glasses re-minds you that children don't always know that things will be okay, that they haven't had enough experience to trust that things will get better. Our ability to tap into their ex-perience and validate what they are feeling not only deep-ens our connection, but also sets the foundation for them navigating future challenges.

Lack of connection makes adults and children feel lonely, and loneliness has nothing to do with being in the presence of others—we could be in a crowded room and feel lonely. It's about feeling connected to ourselves and others, feeling as if we belong and that we have a right to take up space.

Because we depend on one another to survive, feelings of loneliness can feel like actual physical pain. Loneliness for children can be even more painful than it is for adults since they are dependent. They don't have as many options or frames of reference or trust that things will improve. They end up believing the entire world is just like their current situation, lonely and sad, and have difficulty envisioning anything different.

I work with parents who have difficulty communicating with their children because they didn't feel connected to their own parents or have healthy communication role modeled for them. They may have been told that too much attention will spoil children or that strength comes from tackling the world alone, which means not only is there lack of connection, but there's also shame for desiring connection.

Children are not spoiled by connection; it's a positive experience for their emotional and psychological health. We can so easily miss opportunities for connection because instead of listening and responding to our children, we are responding only to our own point of view and failing to relate to their experience. If we can rise to the challenge of understanding rather than telling our kids what they feel and think isn't valid, we deepen the roots of their self-acceptance. This sets the foundation for the parent-child relationship and leads to the ability to practice healthy communication and connection in every relationship going forward.

## Reestablishing Our Roots

The root chakra holds our basic needs for survival, asking the question *Do I belong here?* If we want our children to believe they belong, we first need to know that we belong.

In psychologist Erik Erickson's stages of development, the first stage, trust versus mistrust, is closely related to root-chakra development. If your caregivers provided what you needed as an infant, such as food, water, love, and touch, then you felt secure and that the world was a place to be trusted. But if your environment was chaotic or caregivers were emotionally unavailable, then this trust may be underdeveloped. Whether you feel secure now is often impacted by how safe you felt as a small child.

The awareness of what you didn't have growing up is the first step toward change. Maybe your parents kept you fed and with a roof over your head, but they weren't there for you emotionally. You are not disrespecting them by realizing what you didn't get, and you aren't discounting what you did. You are just recognizing a pattern that you may not want to perpetuate, and it doesn't need to be a public declaration, only an internal realization.

The goal is to break the cycle of mistrust by allowing your children to feel safe and seen in their home. It's like planting a seed with the best possible soil and remembering to water it so it grows strong and with healthy roots. But to nurture them, you also need to nurture yourself. If you want your children to believe they are worthy of belonging, they need to know that you believe this about yourself, too.

Make it a priority to invest in your own sense of "beingness" by choosing relationships that make you feel safe and by making self-care a daily experience. Talk therapy or body work may allow you to work through some old beliefs or untruths, and having a daily gratitude practice can actually change the hard wiring of the brain over time, allowing you to recognize what's working more often.

Scientists say the odds of us being born are at least 1 in 400 trillion, which makes being born incredibly unlikely, almost to the point of impossible. This number alone should tell us all that we belong, that simply being here justifies our worth and necessity. But we have to choose this way of thinking and decide how to write our life stories. If we were given early messages that we were unlovable, we can practice unlearning them by loving ourselves and offering that to others. If we were told that we weren't as good as others, we can practice letting this go by living what we value.

We get to decide how to write our stories, and because we are adults and not dependent children, we have the ability to find ways to write them successfully. Scientists at Yale University followed adults for 20 years to uncover the secrets to a long life, and what they found was that those who had a positive view of aging in midlife lived an average of 7.6 years longer than those who had a negative view. In other words, if you say, "I think getting older will be wonderful," you're likely to live 7.6 years longer than the person who says, "I think getting older is horrible."[8]

Hundreds of research studies demonstrate the influence of a productive story, and the single biggest predictor is not the facts of the situation but the story that is being told about what happened.[9] If you had a difficult childhood or you've had more than your share of trauma, it doesn't mean you are destined to be a disconnected parent. You can instead choose to see your past experiences as information about what you don't want so you can have access to what you do. Your past becomes motivation and an awareness about what you want right now.

One of the best messages of Alcoholics Anonymous is *to live one day at a time*, and in parenting it can be more like *one moment at a time*. We get to choose in every interaction whether we are going to regress to the old patterning of our childhood and limiting beliefs or are going to choose patience and connection when relating to ourselves and our kids.

The process of making moment-to-moment choices to listen to, connect with, and validate our children not only shapes their minds but also reshapes ours. Our story about what we want develops our foundation, and the ability to practice what we want strengthens it. There will be missteps and challenges, but they are also part of the process because they strengthen our ability to be accountable for our behavior by repairing or apologizing if necessary.

The root chakra comprises whatever creates stability in your life: your basic needs, your right to be, the story you tell yourself and others. Kelly McGonigal, author of *The Upside of Stress*, says, "Small shifts in mindset can trigger a cascade of changes so profound that they test the limits of what seems possible."[10] Test those limits and build a sturdy foundation, for your sense of self and for your children.

## For You

* Reflect on the stability of your childhood and home: Did you feel safe? Was home a sanctuary? Are your repeating the patterns of your childhood, or have you created something new?

* Find ways to make the home calmer—visually, emotionally, verbally. Create spaces in the home where you can relax.

* Practice connecting by considering your child's experience rather than telling them how they should feel. Take off your "adult glasses" and remember how the world and experiences can feel to a child or teen.

* Consider your own sense of belonging. Do you feel that you matter, that you have something to offer, that who you are is valuable? If not, make

this understanding a priority. To teach belonging, you have to understand belonging because our kids learn by watching how we live.

## For Your Kids

* Ask your kids how they feel when they come home from school. Does home make them less nervous or more nervous than school? Ask them how much time they need to decompress or how they would like to communicate when they get home after a long day.

* Talk to your kids about calm spaces in the home, including their room. Ask if they need help making their room or study spaces less chaotic and offer your assistance in organizing, purging, or decorating to create a more serene environment (but let them take the lead; you are there to help). This is less about buying new things and more about clearing space so they have an area where they can chill.

* Listen more and talk less when your children are sharing their experiences. Connection occurs when someone feels heard, seen, and understood, and not every conversation necessitates advice or learning.

\* Talk to your kids about what it means to belong.
  It's not just about being a part of a group; it's
  about knowing that who you are is who you are
  supposed to be. It's about reminding them that
  their skills and personality are exactly what the
  world needs. Start by reminding them why they
  are so important in your family, and that sense of
  belonging will be the foundation for their future
  experiences.

Chakra Two

# THE RIGHT TO FEEL

*Being Creative, Accessing
Emotions, Experiencing Pleasure*

Lower abdomen, womb

## ORANGE

What makes the engine go? Desire, desire, desire.

—**STANLEY KUNITZ,** *"Touch Me"*

### Pleasure

The second chakra, sometimes called the sacral chakra or *svadhisthana,* is located at the lower abdomen. *Svadhisthana* is a Sanskrit word that means "one's own abode" or "take pleasure in." This chakra is associated with the emotional body, sexuality, and creativity, and its element is water because it's characterized by flow and flexibility. The function of the sacral chakra is directed by the principle of pleasure, but to embrace it fully the definition of pleasure must be clearly defined.

Depending on how we were raised, pleasure may bring up feelings of shame, guilt, or wasted time. We even have the saying "guilty pleasure" when we are referring to things we enjoy, as if enjoying things should cause guilt. Pleasure, defined as "a feeling of happy satisfaction or enjoyment," is the acknowledgment and appreciation of things that are meaningful to us. Human beings are hardwired to seek pleasure and avoid pain, so it's completely natural to desire pleasurable feelings.

There is nothing inherently bad about seeking pleasure, but there is discernment to why and how we incorporate it into our lives. Even discussing this can get tricky, especially for women, because historically, and even in the current day, our society aims to curb and control women's pleasure. Pleasure is often seen as dangerous or morally problematic, and the only way to make it acceptable is to control it.

Women are taught that too much pleasure may bring social disgrace, so it has to be measured and portioned. You can have sex, but only the right kind of sex with the right kind of people. You can eat food, but only a little of it at the right time and only if you stay thin.

Men are not typically socialized to question or control pleasure, and they are often taught to make pleasure, especially sexual pleasure, the most important thing. Generally, among men, there is less shame in overeating or overdrinking, and they may even become points of pride.

There are exceptions to every rule, so of course men can experience feeling shame for overindulgence, but societally speaking, it is women who are usually taught that they must earn or balance pleasure, and this pressure often leads to more guilt and shame around what they struggle to manage.

Guilt is about feeling bad about a *choice*, while shame is feeling bad about who we *are*. Guilt can be effective in allowing us to learn and grow from our choices, but shame is the belief we are inherently broken and unfixable. When it comes to pleasure, both guilt and shame are difficult to navigate, because we can feel guilty about making a pleasurable choice, even if it's a good choice, like resting instead of overworking. And the act of repeatedly making a pleasurable choice, even a healthy one, can lead to feeling shame for desiring the pleasure. It becomes a vicious cycle of believing that we aren't worthy of enjoyment and that there is something wrong with us for wanting it.

Professionally speaking, many of the women I've worked with hide books, magazines, or television shows they watch for fear of being ridiculed. They turn down pieces of cake in public so they don't appear gluttonous but may turn to overeating in private. They desire emotional and physical connection but feel uncomfortable or simply incapable of asking for what they want sexually. Women also tend to feel guilty for prioritizing fun and pleasure over work and family responsibilities, which leads to their playing the martyr role or hiding essential parts of themselves from the people they love most.

These are examples and not absolutes, but what's most important is that for all genders, pleasure does not have to be earned. Our body and mind were created to desire and appreciate what feels good. Our capacity to experience physical, mental, and emotional pleasure is a birthright and gift to enjoy, and denying it only leads to the guilt-shame cycle.

Our work is to explore what brings us pleasure, because it may be different from typical societal norms. The whole advertising business is built around telling us what *should* give us pleasure, like beauty products, a bigger home, the most expensive restaurants, but real pleasure is very personal; it's about tapping into what's true for you.

Pleasure can mean taking walks in nature or staying inside to read. It can mean enjoying parties with a lot of people or spending a weekend alone. It can be drinking coffee in the morning or having hot tea at night. Owning what feels like pleasure is the first step toward claiming who you are and what you want.

The most vital understanding is that pleasure is about treating yourself well and not about numbing yourself. Eating cake and enjoying how great it tastes is pleasure; eating cake to run away and dull painful emotions is not. Having sex that is mutual while present and engaged is pleasure; having sex that is unwanted, disconnected, or a tool for validation is not. Pleasure is about being fully present and alive in the moment; it's about choosing and appreciating pleasure to enhance your life experience.

For children, pleasure comes through closeness, play, and validation of the emotional experience. Children take pleasure in simply being alive, and then they reach out to the world with that sense of aliveness. Our ability to meet this aliveness with love and encouragement is in itself a pleasurable experience for our children, and it allows us to develop a sense of trust and connection with them where they feel seen and understood.

If we tell children that pleasure is indulgent and a waste of time and energy, or that pleasure is a distraction from hard work and that there are more important ways to spend their time, it can lead to their feeling guilty about doing things they enjoy or cause them to hide parts of themselves they feel ashamed for wanting. And if our children grow up watching us push away pleasure or feeling guilty about having pleasurable experiences, we are demonstrating through our behavior that pleasure is not valued.

Pleasure can also get wrapped up in manipulation, where pleasure is available only if a child "behaves." All pleasure, like hugs, treats, or activities, may get denied if a child is sad or angry, or we may push them away and insist they go to their room until they "get their act together." This can lead to a child denying their difficult emotional states because they fear rejection or not getting what they want.

When pleasure is denied, it makes a person feel as if they are missing a vital ingredient of their humanity. The denial of pleasure leads to a disowning of our right to it, which leads to our feeling guilty about wanting it and ashamed when we have it. Then it's difficult to know what we want or why, and we lose track of our ability to assess what actually feels good and right.

This doesn't mean that we give in to every pleasure or we offer every pleasure to our children; it means that we understand that it's okay to feel pleasure and not feel guilty about what we want. If a child has one cookie and then asks for another, or has an hour of screen time and then asks for more, you can relate to their desire without shaming them. You can let them know you understand their wants while also guiding them to find healthy boundaries and limits.

The goal is to relate to pleasure in a healthy way, to enjoy it as one of the best parts of being human rather than as our weakness we are trying to avoid. Our brain desires things beyond pleasure—such as learning, growth, connection, curiosity—so we can allow pleasure to have its place and trust that the other desires will influence our life choices just as much.

It's only when we deny pleasure that it becomes dark or shame filled, often taking up too much space as something we need to hide. But if we can give healthy pleasure its rightful space, it can lead to a natural balance with all of our other life demands.

## Emotional Intelligence

Early parenting choices tend to focus around a child's intellectual ability, from teaching them to read to finding the best preschool or playgroup. This continues as they age, with excessive focus on grades and test scores or experiences that will enhance their ability to find the "right" college. Educational experiences are important in helping children make sense of the world, but it's just as important, if not more so, to help children make sense of their inner worlds.

The term *emotional intelligence*, first coined by psychologists Peter Salovey and John Mayer, then made mainstream by Daniel Goleman's 1995 book, *Emotional Intelligence: Why It Can Matter More than IQ*, refers to a person's ability to be aware, regulate, and share emotions and then use this ability to understand and relate to others. Emotions are our internal guidance system, so understanding them and how they work is essential for processing and navigating our inner and outer experiences.

Goleman explains that our view of human intelligence is far too narrow and that standardized tests are designed to screen a person's ability to process information but are not an indicator of future life success. According to Goleman, IQ contributes to only 20 percent of success, and the other 80 percent, things like self-motivation, persistence, resilience, self-regulation, and the ability to experience empathy, humor, and hope, falls under EQ.[1]

Children can be taught to identify and communicate their feelings from a very young age, and in a trusted environment where emotions are accepted, kids learn to speak freely about their feelings so they can process and understand their experience. The ability to normalize and validate a child's feelings is not only essential for their own mental well-being but also how they develop empathy for others.

Many of us are taught that some feelings are "good" and some are "bad," but in reality, all feelings are important and have purpose. Avoiding emotions deemed "bad" buys short-term gain at the price of long-term pain. It's detrimental to not acknowledge the whole range of emotions, and pushing them away doesn't get rid of them; it just forces them to morph into something different, like negative behavior, physical pain, or feelings of helplessness.

Repressing or denying difficult emotions can also lead to addictive behaviors such as drinking, drugs, vaping, or more socially typical behaviors such as excessive screen time or constant productivity. The inability or unwillingness to feel difficult feelings also numbs the ability to feel what's good. As vulnerability researcher Brené Brown explains, "You can't numb those hard feelings without numbing the other affects, our emotions. You cannot selectively numb—so when we numb those, we numb joy, we numb gratitude, we numb happiness."[2]

Yet so many families struggle to talk about emotions, or if they do they focus on trying to dismiss them. There is a societal discomfort with sadness, anger, grief, and other feelings associated with pain, so kids are told to "look on the bright side," "suck it up," or "be strong" by avoiding anything other than happiness.

Many of us grew up being told to stop crying or that we didn't have a right to be angry. We spent all of our time trying to avoid or diminish what we felt, and since *what we resist persists,* big feelings eventually win, leaving us to feel out of control or broken. As adults we have to reevaluate the purpose and necessity of emotional expression so we can unlearn what we were told to repress.

This is why we struggle so much when our children are in pain—because we love them and don't want to see them hurt, but also because their pain brings up our own. We feel uncomfortable with what they are feeling because we haven't learned how to feel it ourselves. So instead of allowing our children to express their feelings openly, we tell them that they're okay (even while they are crying or telling us they are not okay), or to quiet down, or that they need to be "brave," when in reality the bravest thing they can do is openly and honestly express what they are feeling.

We need to break the cycle of emotional avoidance so our children trust that feelings are natural and necessary and that they have the ability to process them in a healthy way. As parents we can help them understand the boundaries of what's acceptable. It's okay to be angry, but it isn't okay to hit someone. It's okay to be sad, but it's not okay to blame or scold everyone else for your sadness. The goal is not to take away a child's pain, but to nonjudgmentally be with them as they feel it and then help them learn how to safely let it go. As children's television personality Mr. Rogers said, "People have said, 'Don't cry' to other people for years and years and all it has ever meant is, 'I'm too uncomfortable when you show your feelings, don't cry.' I'd rather have them say, 'Go ahead and cry. I'm here to be with you.'"[3]

Being able to feel our feelings and express them in a healthy way is not only good and cathartic for us but also important role modeling for our kids. Children take their cues from us, so if we act as if we are never sad, disappointed, or angry, our children end up questioning or discounting their own feelings. But if they know that all people, especially the ones they love the most, experience the full range of emotions, it normalizes and validates their experience.

**If we accept and practice feeling our emotions, we give our kids permission to do the same.** Then we can teach them to understand and listen to the messages contained within the emotion. Anger can teach us about our boundaries and what we believe needs to change. Sadness can demonstrate the depth of love we have for ourselves, others, and the world. Disappointment tells us that we tried something and cared deeply about the outcome, and anxiety reminds us that we need to be more present rather than focusing on the past and future.

Our feelings act as internal arrows, pointing out what matters most and what may need to change. Our ability to understand and process our internal states allows us to feel more connected to ourselves and more capable of navigating relationships and the outside world.

As a child, I was very sensitive to the world, and I had a lot of feelings, many of them scary and stressful. One of the people who taught me that I was safe and okay was Mr. Rogers. My mom has told me many times that she knew he made an impact on me, that him telling me that I was valued and special on a daily basis really confirmed something I needed to hear.

I have since studied psychology, neurobiology, and numerous spiritual traditions and have found the emotional intelligence demonstrated by Mr. Rogers is exactly what children and adults need to thrive. All people want to know three things: *Do you see me, do you hear me, and do I matter?* And on an everyday basis, Mr. Rogers answered that question with a resounding *yes.* He pointed out the beauty and joy in the world, but he wasn't solely focused on feeling good; he also shone a light on the normalcy of pain and disappointment. He talked about childhood fears, differences, and shattered lives. He told kids the truth about their experience and allowed them to feel their pain while also being held with love and respect.

To this day I believe that someone like Fred Rogers is the best of who we can all be, a human being who *practiced* being present and kind. As a parent I shared Mr. Rogers with my kids, but, even more important, I look to his example whenever I feel unsure of what to do next. The answers are consistent: tell the truth, be human, be compassionate toward yourself, and treat all people, especially children, with dignity.

As parents this gives us permission to be imperfect and show up as ourselves. Our children should never be expected to take care of us, but we can be honest about our emotions and role model what to do in difficult situations. We can demonstrate how we cry or ask for help, how we practice meditation, prayer, or journaling. We might even demonstrate how we use optimism or humor to get through difficulty. We can point out the beauty of the world and also the injustice, the amazingness of being human and also the limitations.

We can question and point out the false dichotomy that feelings, experiences, or people are just good or bad. This fails to recognize that growth and learning often come from mistakes, missteps, and pain. That's why forgiveness and resilience are values that need to be discussed and practiced.

Nothing is clean-cut and things are rarely simple, so I make a point to talk to my kids about seeing the gray and acknowledging the paradox of every situation. The more we accept that both light and dark exist in all things, the more we can stop fighting or hiding what is. Feeling envious or jealous can feel uncomfortable and at times even lead to shame, but jealousy and envy are also indicators of what we value or what we would like to achieve. Even uncomfortable emotions can shine a light on what we desire and allow us to get more in touch with ourselves.

Relating to our inner workings offers us a full picture that can't be limited to just good or bad. The messages inside our emotional experiences offer us information and a road map for what comes next, allowing us to embrace all aspects of ourselves and teach our children to do the same.

## Creativity and Play

Creativity is our ability to be inventive, imaginative, and innovative; it's the privilege of being original about the way we live our lives. At a young age all children embrace their uniqueness and are clearly creative and imaginative, but at some point, usually in elementary or middle school, there is a weeding-out process that decides which children are more creative than others. This is usually based on competitions or awards for best drawing, writing, or singing, and if you don't find yourself noticed or chosen, it's assumed there is a lack of what's necessary to be deemed creative.

Yet all humans are innately creative throughout their lives, and it's the early education experiences that can sidetrack us by making competitive artwork more important than our inborn desire to express ourselves. Elizabeth Gilbert, author of *Big Magic*, describes creativity as "living a life that is driven more strongly by curiosity than by fear" and "as a devotional practice, as an act of love, and as a lifelong commitment to the search for grace and transcendence."[4]

Our ability to redefine creativity as personal expression offers the freedom to worry less about comparison and more about what makes us feel like us. And it's not just about drawing or singing; it's about the way we choose to think, dress, speak, or cook or where we decide to spend our time—it's the way we show up and contribute to the world. Creativity is the sense of meaning and fulfillment we all yearn for but not enough of us actualize.

Because creativity is the act of cultivating meaning, our ability to let go of comparison is our most necessary and self-compassionate act. Again, the majority of educational experiences set us up to think that everything is about comparison, that being first or best is the only way to succeed. But in adulthood we have the independence to think differently and finally show up as ourselves. Being ourselves is, in itself, success, and as Ralph Waldo Emerson said, "To be yourself in a world that is constantly trying to make you something else is the greatest accomplishment."[5]

Brené Brown's research demonstrated that creative living necessitates the willingness to embrace vulnerability. This is difficult for people who need constant control or need to be perceived as perfect, but the alternative risks our emotional well-being. Dr. Brown found that "unused creativity is not benign. It metastasizes and turns into grief, rage, judgment, sorrow, shame."[6]

Being creative is important for our sense of self, but the outcome of our creativity is less important. As Gilbert explains, "Creativity is sacred, and it is not sacred. What we make matters enormously, and it doesn't matter at all."[7] Creativity gives us the opportunity to live out loud and enjoy the expression minus the need for external validation.

When I was in my early forties, I decided to take a beginner's tap-dance class on Thursdays and a regular dance class on Saturday morning. I did both when I was young, but at this point it was like starting over. It was hard, but I *loved* it—the process, the nostalgia, the learning without needing to prove anything or be better than anybody else. I started trying more and fearing less, and as a mom of three kids, dancing was an escape that was just for me; it brought me back to myself.

Individually, we need to find what speaks to us, like writing poetry for pleasure or making pottery just for enjoyment, singing without needing to be part of a choir or decorating our homes in our aesthetic. If any of our creative endeavors turn into something that involves compensation or getting noticed, that's just icing on the cake.

Creativity is also about our ability to just have fun and play. Being imaginative, curious, and silly always feels good, and while our society teaches us that adulthood and maturity mean moving past play, Dr. Stuart Brown, head of the National Institute for Play, found that play in adulthood is just as important. Dr. Brown describes play as "something done for its own sake—it's voluntary, it's pleasurable, it offers a sense of engagement, it takes you out of time. And the act itself is more important than the outcome."[8]

Play helps us maintain our social well-being, through the joy of board games, sports leagues, roller coasters, or waterslides. My husband is always up for play; he even keeps balls, gloves, and Frisbees in each of our cars just in case he gets the opportunity. He forces all of us to participate in games during the holidays or couples get-togethers because he knows that play is how we connect. His made-up games get us out of our day-to-day lives and remind us to be present.

Children are experts in reminding us why play is important, mostly because it feels like joy and looks like fun (the best reasons ever). It wakes us up to what we have forgotten and reminds us to pay attention to what feels good. Simple things like dressing up for Halloween or turning up the music and singing in the car reconnect us to the part of ourselves that longs for more expression and joy.

In Randy Pausch's book *The Last Lecture*, he talks about how he asked his parents if he could draw and paint the walls of his bedroom, and to his surprise they said yes. He took that opportunity to paint his walls with things that mattered to him—dreams, jokes, interests, and hobbies. He was able to express himself and live in a room where his expression was reflected back. He passed away from cancer in 2008, but he said that his parents never painted over the walls and that it was their favorite room to show when they were giving a tour of the house. Dr. Pausch wrote, "Anybody out there who is a parent, if your kids want to paint their bedrooms, as a favor to me, let them do it. It will be OK. Don't worry about resale value on the house. I don't know how many more times I will get to visit my childhood home. But it is a gift every time I go there."[9]

## Sexuality

Chakra two is located near the reproductive organs, governing our sexuality. The second chakra inhabits all of our different drives: sex, desire, courtship, reproduction, family, and companionship, and while the first chakra is about survival, the second is connected to seeking pleasure in all of its forms, including sex.

As a sex educator to fifth and eighth graders in several parochial schools in Chicagoland, I am given an opportunity to talk with the parents before I talk with the kids. There is so much discomfort around sex education, and every year parents nervously ask how I will cover certain topics or handle difficult questions. I assure them that I will use developmentally appropriate honesty. The fifth graders usually just want a simple answer about why men's and women's bodies are different, why twins are born, or why anyone would want to have sex in the first place, but the eighth graders need more specific information about how the body works, the consequences of their decision making, and whether it's normal to have certain feelings or desires.

I focus on the body parts and mechanics, but I also talk about the emotional and spiritual aspects of sex. I talk to kids *and* adults about how sex is not just a physical experience, but also an experience that impacts all aspects of our being. This is important for kids to understand so they aren't easily duped into believing that sexual activity is "no big deal" and also for parents to understand so they know how important it is to talk to kids about sex from a very young age and into adulthood.

I am using the words *sex* and *sexuality* interchangeably, but typically when I teach I explain that *sexuality* is the big picture of our sexual nature: how we identify, participate, think, feel, and understand everything that is sexual. *Sex* is sexual acts, including intercourse.

The kids I work with feel so vulnerable and uninformed about their sexuality. As adults we have amnesia about how much support we needed when it came to sexuality, how much time we spent believing there was something wrong with us or that we should feel ashamed for being confused or having normal questions.

When I work with adult clients, I tend to hear, "Why do I need to talk about sex with my kids? Nobody talked to me, and I turned out fine." My follow-up question is *Is that true?* Do you feel comfortable in your body, do you feel as if you have a healthy sex life, and do you feel freedom in being a sexual being?

If not, then maybe communication, education, and some support might have been helpful, might still be helpful, even today. Many of us were given a book or two when we were young, but so few of us were given the opportunity to ask questions without judgment or offered information when we most needed it. Instead, we were often shamed for being curious and left to figure it out for ourselves.

Our culture is obsessed with sex, yet we act as if it's too taboo to discuss. Since my children were little, they've been driven by billboards with half-naked women on them, they've looked at magazines that objectify women and men, and they've watched movies and television shows that are either overtly sexual or meant to be funny based on sexual innuendo.

Our culture shows children sex every day through social networking and every type of media, and it's our job as parents to help them wade through all of this information, to help them process what they see and navigate the many aspects of what it means to live in their bodies and live in a society that struggles to discuss sexuality in a healthy way.

This can be difficult for adults who still have difficulty talking about their own sexuality or sexual experiences. Childhood trauma around sex (physical or emotional), religious fear or shaming, or just overall lack of information and perspective when it comes to sex leads to feeling inadequate, shut down, or even addicted to sex in an effort to overcompensate. This means that as parents, we have to do our own work around sexuality, that we need to first get clear about what we were taught and why and if it's helping or hindering our current adult experiences.

Most of my adult female clients struggle with their sex lives, because of body image or because they don't feel they have permission to ask for what they need. Most women are made to feel inadequate based on societal norms regarding beauty, and at a young age they got the message that sex was mostly for men and that it was a woman's job to service rather than receive.

While attitudes have changed and continue to evolve, some of our inner beliefs may not have kept up with the times. It's important to acknowledge our own fears, shame, and limitations when it comes to sex so we can talk to our children from a place of empowerment and confidence.

Sex is always a difficult topic. It's okay if we aren't 100 percent comfortable; we can still acknowledge and rise to the occasion of important sexual discussions, not just one conversation about the "birds and the bees," but ongoing, open communication about what it means to be a sexual human being. These conversations can start early, by first talking about body parts and answering simple questions honestly, and then deepening the education as the kids age.

We can worry less about having the perfect answers and more about being able to have space for the questions. If we don't have an answer to a question, we can tell our kids that what they have asked is important and that we want to think more about our answer before we share. We can ask friends and experts for help, and we can buy books and find websites and offer them to our kids. The goal is to allow for the conversation, to let our kids know that we are nonjudgmentally available and that we are willing and capable of addressing what they want to know.

When I offer sex-education talks for parents, I open by asking, *What do you want to teach your kids about sex, and what are your hopes for their sexual futures?* This question initially gets some laughs and discomfort, but it eventually leads to the awareness that if we haven't thought about what we want to teach, nothing will get taught.

Most parents hope that their children choose a partner they love, that they eventually have healthy sex lives, and that they feel confident with their sexuality. There are other desires as well, some of them more restrictive or more open, but regardless of what values or virtues we want to impart, we have to make sure what we are offering is lining up with our intentions.

The Dutch approach to sex education is probably the most comprehensive, and the Netherlands has some of the best outcomes when it comes to teen sexual health. On average, teens in the Netherlands have sex later than those in other European countries or in the United States. Researchers found that among twelve- to twenty-five-year-olds in the Netherlands, most say they had positive first sexual experiences, whereas 66 percent of sexually active American teens surveyed said they wished that they had waited longer to have sex for the first time.[10]

A Rutgers World Population Foundation study found that nine out of ten Dutch teens used contraceptives the first time, and World Health Organization data show that Dutch teens are among the top users of the birth control pill. According to the World Bank, the teen pregnancy rate in the Netherlands is one of the lowest in the world.[11]

In the United States, where not all states are mandated to teach sex education and an abstinence-only approach is still very common, public health and medical professional organizations, including the American Medical Association, the American Academy of Pediatrics, the American College of Obstetricians and Gynecologists, the American Public Health Association, the American School Health Association, and the Society for Adolescent Health and Medicine, have all rallied around comprehensive sex education due to the research demonstrating that information and access to information result in better, safer, and healthier outcomes for kids and teens.[12]

We can appreciate the education from the school, but it's only a small piece of what kids need. When I teach sex ed, I spend maybe two hours with twenty to twenty-five kids—we get through the bare minimum, and so many kids are left without their questions answered. I suggest that they go home and tell their parents everything we discussed and see if their parents have any questions. It's a way of opening up a discussion that should always remain open.

While every family can formulate a sexual discussion in alignment with their own values, the hope is that it's always approached without shame or judgment, to listen instead of imposing and relate rather than disregard, to use the media, like television shows or magazine covers, as launching points to have important discussions about how sexuality is discussed in our culture and then to use these opportunities to share what you hope your children will know.

*For You*

* Think about what is pleasurable to you. Do you feel guilty about it? Do you hide it or not talk about it? Consider whether you appreciate the pleasure in life and how and why you seek it (for enjoyment, to run away or numb, or a mixture of both).

* Pay attention to your emotional experiences, and maybe even label what you are feeling: disappointed, appreciative, excited, sad. Do your best to not use compilation words like *stressed* or *overwhelmed*—they are too general and do not get to the heart of your feelings. Try more descriptive words like *tired, concerned, lonely, overstimulated, frustrated, embarrassed,* or *discouraged.*

* Think about what types of creative and playful endeavors you enjoyed as a child—painting, singing, dancing, decorating, writing poetry or lyrics, doodling, games, makeup, or taking things apart and creating something new. Consider doing one creative or playful thing every day, even if it's small, to reconnect to that part of yourself without fear of comparison.

* Think about who talked to you about sex or how you learned about sex. Did it lead to positive or poor outcomes? Decide what you want your child to know about sex and sexuality so you can begin discussing your values and what it is you want them to know. Practice short, ongoing discussions instead of one big talk. This keeps the communication open and allows for questions and conversation without fear or judgment.

## For Your Kids

* Allow your children to want or desire without judging or shaming them. You can still say no, set limits, and discuss appropriate boundaries, but stay connected by relating to what they feel rather than telling them what they feel is wrong. Shaming them for wanting leads them to believe there is something inherently wrong with them, while discussing limits and boundaries allows them to consider their needs and make aligned choices.

* Allow your children to express themselves emotionally and offer words to describe their feelings (*You look angry. You seem disappointed. I understand why that would be so exciting . . .*). The more language they have to describe what they feel and

the more they feel understood by you, the less likely they will be to repress or deny their emotional experiences, leading to mental wellness and self-understanding.

* Encourage your child to be creative, just for fun, without any comparison or competition. Dancing around the house doesn't always mean they have to be in a class, and playing ball in the backyard doesn't mean they have to be on a travel team. If they want to participate or compete in a sport or activity, then do your best to support them. But if they just appreciate the joy of moving and playing without expectation, then allow them to have the enjoyment.

* Use the correct words for body parts and discuss puberty way before puberty. Normalize feelings and questions without fear or shame. Discuss partnership without gender specificity, and if your children are older, ask them questions and allow them to educate you about their experiences when it comes to sexuality and gender. Set the stage for an ongoing conversation about sex and sexuality, and allow your children to share and ask questions without judgment or shame.

## Chakra Three

# THE RIGHT TO ACT

*Establishing Our Identity
and Sense of Self*

Solar plexus, abdomen

### YELLOW

There is a vitality, a life force, a quickening that is translated through you into action, and there is only one of you in all time, this expression is unique, and if you block it, it will never exist through any other medium and it will be lost.

—MARTHA GRAHAM, *as quoted in Shane Breslin, "Keep the Channel Open: Martha Graham and a Message for All of Us"*

## Autonomy and the Hero's Journey

The third chakra is located above the navel and below the sternum, often referred to as the solar plexus. It's the source of personal power and self-worth, and it's represented by the fire element and the color yellow, similar to the sun bringing warmth, power, energy, and light. The third chakra is about personal well-being and clarity, the ability to be self-confident and make choices that reflect who you are and what you need.

The chakras are a progression from individuality toward universality, with the first three chakras focusing on a foundational sense of self. Chakra three is the greatest expression of our individual selves and our desire to have a unique and necessary voice in the world.

Autonomy relies on our ability to individuate, to break away from the internalized patterns of our family and culture so we can define who we are. Some families support and expect individuation, but others meet this process with disapproval or control. The people we love most or know best may have their own plans or dreams for us, so the act of individuation feels like a rebellion or a retaliation against them.

Many parents and cultures struggle with reconciling their own dreams with their children's autonomy, but eventually this process is necessary for an individual to align with themselves and their life purpose.

American professor and mythologist Joseph Campbell called this process the Hero's Journey, a classic story structure about self-discovery, where a character ventures out to get what they need, faces conflict, and ultimately triumphs over adversity.

The Hero's Journey can be found in the great religious stories about Christ, Buddha, and Moses and in popular literature such as *A Wrinkle in Time*, *The Hobbit*, and *The Alchemist*. It's also the foundation of classic movies such as *Star Wars*, *The Lion King*, and *The Wizard of Oz*.

The journey is usually in three stages—departure, initiation, and return—with many substages in between. A hero feels a call to adventure, initially refuses the call, but then sets out on a road of trials that inform and deepen the understanding and belief in self. Then the hero returns home changed, and who they were born to be is revealed and offered to the world.

These stories are fables, but the path they reveal carries essential truth for everyone. Every person is meant to evolve into who they were born to be. This is not always about finding a career or hobby; it's about self-discovery on the path to personal understanding and power. It's about taking responsibility for one's life by making decisions, having clarity of judgment, and discovering a confidence and self-assurance about who you are and what you want.

I have had so many different kinds of hero's journeys throughout my life, some small and some more life altering. In middle school, I recognized that my choices were leading me in the wrong direction, so I changed how I spoke and acted, even going a whole year without swearing.

In high school, I had to navigate academics and some of my most important relationships. In college when I left home for the first time, I had to completely start over, as I did when I lived in Chicago by myself while going to school and working full-time.

These were just a few of the events that significantly altered my early life experiences, and in adulthood I continued to have challenges that led me into a journey of self-discovery. Identity loss as a new mom, depression and anxiety, miscarriages, the chronic illness of my mom, and the death of my dad were just some of the things that led to dark nights of the soul and awakenings that allowed me to live much closer and truer to myself.

I have had to unlearn so much of what I thought was truth; I have had to acknowledge that so many of my choices and behaviors had been based in fear. I have had to learn how to speak up for my needs and take up space in a room. I have had to let go of overapologizing and people pleasing because I thought that was the only way I would be loved or accepted.

This is an ongoing process, not a onetime recognition. And just when I think I have dealt with an issue for the last time, it shows up again. As Oprah Winfrey said in her Stanford commencement speech, "If you don't get the lesson, it shows up wearing different pants."[1] Sometimes things need to be learned a few times, and sometimes the same thing has a lot of layers, like an onion that needs to be peeled over a lifetime.

## Individuation

Our ability to recognize our own power and autonomy allows us to take responsibility for ourselves and make the necessary changes to create different outcomes. If we cannot see ourselves as separate from others, then we are incapable of taking responsibility for our actions. This can lead to our acting passively and irresponsibly, leaving us to complain about our circumstances and relationships because we feel powerless to make any kind of change.

If we have not individuated, then we may spend our lives blaming others. The inability to take responsibility for our lives strips us of our personal power, which means everybody else is the problem. This keeps us stuck in a pattern of fighting others and the world instead of harnessing our own ability to create change.

Carl Jung, one of the pioneers of modern psychology and psychoanalysis, described individuation as an essential life goal, a discovery of one's life purpose. Jung saw individuation as a process that largely occurs in the second half of life, while Margaret Mahler, a twentieth-century psychiatrist who studied children's development, described individuation as a process that begins in early childhood, when a child recognizes the self as an individual separate from the primary caregiver.

Mahler described this process as a "psychological birth" that unfolds over several phases and that eventually results in the development of the infant's ego, sense of identity, and cognitive abilities. This is similar to what happens in adolescence, which is often called the "second phase" of separation individuation, where the adolescent must learn to self-regulate and self-define so they can begin to trust their ability to survive and thrive as an independent adult.

Individuation is an innate desire and drive, a necessary process to develop the ability to function in the world independently. This is why parents need to be aware and open to their children speaking up for themselves and negotiating their own needs and boundaries. It usually starts around the twos and threes ("I do it myself!") and continues into the teenage years, when kids are discovering their own sense of style through things like clothes, activities, and music choices.

Individuation can be difficult for the parent, because if not understood, it can feel like rebellion against family norms or previous childhood interests. New likes and discoveries may be viewed as not acceptable, not "like them," or treated as disrespect or disloyalty. But it's a developmental process of self-discovery, a way for a child to back away from what they already know so they can figure out what feels right today.

There is a way to support our children through this individuation process, to watch with curiosity and listen to what they need to express. We can take an interest in their new interests and even allow them to teach us about what they are learning. We can set up boundaries to keep them safe, like setting curfews or having an expectation of communicating before making major life decisions, but we can also stand back enough to let them find their own way and discover their own sense of self.

An inability to allow our children this time for discovery may have roots in our own powerlessness as children. In the process of individuation, we transition from the family's ways of viewing the world to becoming our own people with distinct perspectives. If we were not allowed to do this, or if shame and judgment were used to make us conform to our parents' worldview, we may be unconsciously continuing this pattern of control with our kids.

To raise children who trust themselves, we must first pay attention to our own individuation, or lack of individuation, so we can reclaim our personal power. If we were not given permission to individuate during childhood, we can acknowledge that we now have the space and security to do so. We are no longer dependent on and vulnerable to caregivers, so we can choose to recognize our own needs and wants.

Once we know what individuation and personal power look and feel like (even in the smallest amounts, like identifying our favorite color or favorite movie), it makes it easier to offer this kind of freedom to our children. Once we know ourselves as individuals, it becomes easier to allow our children to find themselves without guilt or judgment.

If up to this point we have been controlling our children's lives—deciding what they wear, what activities they are in, or even telling them how they should feel—it can feel scary to let go and allow them to choose for themselves. Because of our own history or sense of feeling unsupported in individuating, we may have mistaken support for control, micromanaging their lives so much that they will eventually feel suffocated or enmeshed with our needs.

Gently and slowly, we can allow our kids to reclaim their choices and speak their opinions. Just allowing them to vocalize how they feel or see the world without judgment is a step toward their individuation. In the moment it can feel difficult to trust the unfolding of their self-wisdom and their life choices, but with hindsight it will be easy to see how every new experience, even the challenging ones, led to their developing strength and confidence.

No matter what we do, there are no guarantees. There will be scary and uncertain moments, and there will be sadness and pain because a lived life includes light and dark. Our children will have their own challenges and inevitably make missteps, and so will we. But every misstep is an opportunity to learn together, to realize that we can always choose differently, reframe what we are experiencing, and grow stronger and wiser.

I still find myself trying to hold my teenage daughter's hand as we cross the street, and when my oldest daughter is driving, I can be an annoying backseat driver, pointing out stop signs and pedestrians crossing as if she doesn't have the ability to see them.

I know that as a parent, it's my job to show up, but another part of my job is to practice backing off. A difficult, but essential, parenting skill is to know when to stop lecturing and start listening. The more we listen to what our children are saying, the more we will understand their unique needs and inner workings. Individuation depends on our children's ability to succeed on their own terms, and to support them through this process we have to listen to what they say they need, not what *we think* they need.

We also need to trust that our children are hardwired to be resilient. They have an innate ability and intrinsic drive to get back up, even after a hard fall. It's through the most painful and unexpected experiences that they develop a sense of humility, along with resilience and compassion for themselves and others.

We want to shield our kids from pain, and in some instances we can. But we cannot, or should not, hover over their lives and make their choices (often called "helicopter parenting"), and we shouldn't continuously move things out of the way so they don't have any obstacles (often called "snowplow parenting"). Instead, we can teach them to trust themselves so they can understand and process their feelings. And instead of thinking we should or can feel for them, we can sit in the dark with them and trust that they have the capacity to manage what's happening.

One of my favorite visuals is to envision my child on a balance beam. When my daughter was really little, she needed my hand and close attention to not fall off the beam, so I stayed close and held her hand to ensure her safety. But as she grew and learned more, I needed to let go and stand back so she could discover her own balance without my interference.

As she continues to grow, I stand back even more, but stay close enough so she knows I am there. If she falls and asks for assistance to get back up, I can help. If she stumbles and needs only a gentle nod of "You can do it" from me, then I can do that, too. What we both know is that life is about understanding and mastering this balance beam and that she needs to trust her ability and know that I trust her ability, too.

Mastering this beam will never be done perfectly, but it can be, as pediatrician and psychoanalyst Donald W. Winnicott described, "good enough." *Good-enough parenting* is the understanding that you are bringing your children into an imperfect world and that you yourself are not perfect, but human. Part of psychological wellness is accepting that none of us is perfect. Once we accept this about ourselves, we can accept this about our children, and in turn they accept this about us.

A *good-enough parent* supports their children in accepting frustration, becoming self-sufficient, and learning how to self-soothe. A *good-enough parent* also allows their children to discover their own interests and choose their likes and dislikes. A *good-enough parent* understands and allows for an imperfect process of individuation, even though it can be uncertain or uncomfortable. Watching our children grow up and become their own people is filled with both immense joy and grief, an all-encompassing, fully human experience.

## Self-Care

"I am a Self" is an excellent third chakra mantra, because it's where we hold our ability to recognize, support, and advocate for our needs. Knowing ourselves in this way determines our ability to accurately represent ourselves to others and live in the healthiest and most authentic way.

To be healthy, care of the self is nonnegotiable. We attribute self-care to getting a manicure or going on vacation, but it's much more in-depth, essential, and ongoing. It's the ability to pay attention and take care of our mental, emotional, and physical health. A simple concept in theory, it can be easily overlooked and too often viewed as selfish or a luxury.

Taking responsibility for being healthy is the opposite of selfish; it's actually the only way we can learn to manage our lives and care for others. As a new mom, I was shocked at how quickly my self-care suffered, at how taking care of my baby led to my living on autopilot, forgetting to shower, eat, or ask for any help.

The culture shock of it all led to a big identity crisis and low-grade depression. I thought focusing all of my energy and attention on my daughter was the right thing to do, but ignoring my needs left me depleted, with a lot of painful feelings of loss and loneliness. I didn't know much at the time, but I knew this couldn't be good for either of us.

Discovering self-care started with difficult conversations. Talking to my husband about how I felt and figuring out how we could coparent, rather than have everything fall to me, was the big first step. This was many years ago before we were having cultural discussions about emotional labor and the invisible labor of women, so it felt radical and deeply uncomfortable to discuss why I shouldn't be expected to take care of all things related to the baby. We talked about why I asked if it was okay to leave the house when he left whenever he wanted to. We discussed why I was expected to know everything about the baby, while he didn't know where certain clothes or supplies were even kept.

These ongoing discussions opened both of our eyes, and just speaking these things out loud decreased my resentment. My husband and I were forced to be more honest with each other and communicate more candidly. We still have difficult discussions, because to be completely honest, I still tend to carry more of the emotional/invisible labor. But we are much closer to equal, and the conversation about what each of us needs is always on the table. In the end, my daughter, and eventually her two sisters, had the experience of two primary caregivers and a connected relationship with both mom and dad.

Early on I knew I couldn't be the only one experiencing this baby culture shock, and I wanted to be with other new moms who understood what I was feeling. I decided to create and facilitate a class at our local hospital where new moms met every week and shared the truth. We heard and validated each other, and we discussed how to make ourselves a priority and ask for help.

I also started writing a newsletter that turned into a blog, which eventually became my first book. I found an online graduate program to get my parent-coaching certification, and I started coaching other moms over the phone. Somewhere in the midst of all of these self-care decisions, I started to feel more like myself.

And every moment since, I've worked hard to find some kind of balance. I never strive for perfect balance because that doesn't exist. Instead, it's about feeling too weighted in one direction, where it becomes obvious that attention needs to be paid or an adjustment needs to be made. It's less about finding perfect center and more about getting closer to the middle.

What I know is that I need time alone and also downtime with friends and family. My husband is my partner and the person I talk to the most, but I don't expect him to solve all of my problems. I have a therapist because I am committed to learning more about myself and taking responsibility for my behavior. Just telling her my challenges is in itself cathartic, and learning new tools for self-regulation makes me experience the world differently. I also journal and create vision boards, and I go to bed at a decent time. I've been a yoga student for about twenty years and a yoga teacher for half of that time, and I have a consistent meditation practice.

Some of these things come and go, but a few of them are done daily, not to demonstrate my resolve, but because they are necessary for my emotional well-being and almost medicinal in nature. Without meditation and yoga, I can easily fall into old patterns of thinking, and I don't feel as good physically. When I'm on vacation, I can find things to take their place (walks, unstructured time for reading and relaxing), but when I'm in my regular day-to-day routine, they are necessary for my stability.

I know from my own personal and professional experience that self-care is an emotional necessity. It's a personal responsibility that allows us to participate in life in a healthy way, to show up to our jobs and show up for our families. My relationship and interactions with my partner and children are dependent on my ability to practice self-care.

At the very same time, self-care does not protect us from challenges or keep us from difficulty. Some of my clients use self-care in an almost superstitious way, like if they forget to meditate, they are inviting something bad into their lives. Self-care is not perfectly balanced; some days are better than others, and it never keeps us from having life experiences. Instead, it allows us to function and deal with our life experiences. We can do every type of self-care imaginable and still struggle at times, and if we don't accept this, we will shame and judge ourselves, believing that we are failures rather than just human.

Daily struggles and life challenges will throw things out of balance, and no matter what I do, my emotions and energy will fluctuate, just like any other human being. But I would rather those days be the exception rather than the rule. My family should not have to walk on eggshells around me, and they should not be the recipients of my unacknowledged pain. My family deserves to feel safe and supported in their home and not at the mercy of my mood.

The only way my children will learn how to take care of themselves is if they see me doing it. If I am role modeling personal responsibility and self-care, they will see these things as typical rather than a luxury. If they witness my self-compassion, they will know that it's necessary and normal to feel it for themselves. Children learn what's acceptable by watching how people live, so it's in our best interests, and theirs, to show them how we make ourselves a priority.

## Energy

Having an understanding of our energy and how it affects others is an essential part of our third-chakra awareness. When we are in conflict, it's very easy to blame someone else. It requires self-reflection to notice the energy we carry into every conversation and how what we bring determines the response and outcome.

This is one of the most important conversations that I have with parents, and initially they feel blamed for anything negative that happens in the home. Paying attention to our energy is not about self-blame; it's about knowing what we have control over and what we don't. We can't force the person in front of us to change what they are thinking or feeling, but we can take responsibility for our own energy. By shifting our perspective, reaction, or ability to listen, we change the whole conversational dynamic and outcome.

If we do not recognize our own ability and power to make choices and changes, then we will inevitably feel at the mercy of the world and blame everyone else for making our lives difficult. We may also feel entitled to be unkind or irresponsible whenever we so choose but then feel appalled if someone is unkind to or irresponsible with us.

Newton's third law, an indisputable law of physics, states that *for every action, there is an equal and opposite reaction*. This essentially means that whatever we put out there is what we get back. If we approach situations or conversations with angry or fear-based energy, it is natural to experience it in return.

Understanding Newton's law offers us the capability to shift every dynamic simply by paying attention to ourselves. We can monitor our tone of voice and the words we choose to use with our children. We can ask our partner a question with a sense of compassion and openness rather than defensiveness and anger. By taking responsibility for our end of the equation, we have a better chance for respectful discourse.

Our energy and vibes are part of who we are—whether we are at a party, talking on the phone, or writing on social networking platforms. We offer our energy and vibes to everyone we encounter. One of the best examples of this was shared in a TED Talk and eventual book by brain scientist Jill Bolte Taylor, a Harvard-trained scientist who had a massive stroke on the left side of her brain at the age of thirty-seven.

She lost the ability to speak or even remember her own mother, but because the right side of her brain was still intact, she could feel everyone's energy very acutely. She felt it so acutely that she insisted that every doctor, nurse, and visitor who entered her hospital room take responsibility for the energy they brought into her space.

When our left brain is online, it takes up a lot of our processing space with its data managing, language, and computations. Left-brain activities distract us from the energy and vibrations that we are constantly experiencing simultaneously. Even if we aren't thinking about the energy we are experiencing, we are absorbing it unconsciously. It impacts our feelings, responses, and sense of safety. If you've ever walked into a room where you can tell something has gone wrong even without visual proof, or if you've experienced a sense of fear with someone that you've never even met, you are experiencing energy.

It is fairly easy for us to spot this in other people. Some people brighten the room when they enter, and others do it when they leave. We all have that friend or relative who sucks the energy out of every person at gatherings, and even when we know better, we often can't escape fast enough to not feel drained by their presence. We are also aware that watching the news or violent programming can depress or deplete us—but without thinking about it, we continue to turn it on and watch.

We haven't been trained how to stop the behavior because most of us were raised to be "good" and hide our feelings to be pleasing to others. We get so used to being out of touch with our thoughts and emotions that we forget that wherever we go, there we are. We see examples that teach us that other people and circumstances are to blame when we are unhappy or upset, and once we adopt that kind of mindset, we begin to believe that other people and events are the reason for our unhappiness or problems.

The problem with playing the "blame game" is that it keeps us from taking any possible constructive action. By deflecting responsibility, we get to feel righteous with our fear, anger, and pain rather than making any effort to see our role in the situation. Anytime we believe that anything originates outside of ourselves, then we are abdicating responsibility for how we think and act.

Since I was little, I've been aware that I feel other people's energy and feelings very strongly, and as an adult I learned this is referred to as being an *empath*. We all have the ability to feel the energy of others, but for some, including me, it comes much easier. I'm highly attuned to other people's moods, good and bad, and if I'm not careful I end up absorbing other people's feelings. This has consequences, especially when people are experiencing pain and anxiety.

As a human in the world, especially as a therapist, there is no way to avoid other people's painful feelings. And for many years, I had a hard time differentiating between what was mine and what was someone else's. This often led to my feeling sick and overwhelmed, and at one point I had to give up my one-on-one therapeutic practice because I didn't know how to not absorb what my clients were feeling.

Through education and practice I've developed some healthy boundaries, but I remain vigilant because it's always a work in progress. Even when it's challenging, I'm grateful for the experience because it's taught me that we are more than just the words we say or the body language we use. We are responsible for our energy and how we show up to every conversation and interaction; we are capable of making decisions that can benefit our relationships and realign our paths.

## True and False Self

Donald Winnicott, the same therapist who coined the term *good-enough parent*, also studied the true and false self, specifically meaning that people, young and usually unknowingly, develop a false self to protect their inner, more vulnerable, true self.

Winnicott described babies as "spontaneous," meaning that they act on their needs. They cry for help and reach out for reassurance without considering how they will be received, because needing help and reassurance is essential for our true selves.

If parents are doing what they can and are mostly proficient in gratifying the infant and growing child's needs, the child will experience their basic needs and desires as relatable and that what they experience is manageable. A child with this kind of reassurance grows up with a basic ability to share their true self with the world.

But if parents can't respond sufficiently to the physical and emotional needs and reassurance is not given (possibly due to illness, depression, or the demands of others' needs), a child begins to believe that their basic and truest needs are not acceptable or are unmanageable. The child will become what Winnicott calls *compliant*, which means the child will adjust their behavior and no longer ask for what they need.

Compliance is the child's attempt to protect themselves from further inadequacy or disappointment by covering up their original needs and desires. This is where the false self begins.

People with really active false selves can live perfectly successful lives, but they often feel phony or unsatisfied. They can also be overly accommodating to other people's expectations in the hopes of connecting, but they may come across as performative or awkward, resulting in less authentic and less satisfying relationships. Winnicott points out that having a strong false self keeps people from knowing how to act authentically or spontaneously, leaving them feeling disconnected from themselves and not understanding why.

Since our early relationships help form our primary sense of self, relationships can also be the path back to ourselves. The development of healthy relationships with a partner, friend, or even a therapist can begin to untangle our false selves from our true selves so we can find more honest expressions of who we are.

We know our false selves have taken over when everything becomes external, when the focus is on *what I have, what I can achieve, who pays attention, and how I get more.* The false self gets lost in trying to find more, to constantly seek validation from the outside world. It becomes a vicious cycle of needing bigger and better, an incessant and never-ending game of king of the hill.

The true self knows that joy comes from alignment with self and that the place we knew as a baby is what makes us feel most alive. The true self knows what it likes and asks for what it needs. It focuses on what feels authentic and internally comfortable rather than always clamoring for external validation.

The interplay of having a sense of self while understanding and making space for others can be expressed as *The world is not all about me, but I am vital to the world.* We can recognize and adhere to social norms without losing ourselves in the process, and we can honor and recognize all human beings without giving ourselves away. This leads to healthy third-chakra energy, an integrated sense of self that understands it's a vital piece of the greater whole.

*For You*

 * Consider your own hero's journey(s) and how certain events woke you up to who you are and what you are capable of doing and being.

 * Consider whether you were allowed to individuate from your parents or if sharing your opinion or having a different perspective was perceived as disrespectful or disloyal. Consider how this affected you then and how it continues to affect you today.

 * Develop a self-care practice that works for you: a gratitude practice, laughing with a friend, or relaxing and watching a movie you love. Put yourself on the list by incorporating one small or big self-care practice into every day.

 * Pay attention to the energy you bring into every situation and how what you are feeling and saying impacts the outcome of every dynamic.

 * Consider whether you are living authentically from a place of your own integrity or if you feel unsafe to really show up as yourself. Make a list of your favorite things: color, food, song, movie, flower. Think about your choices and whether they reflect your inner self or what you think the world demands.

*For Your Kids*

* Hold space for your children's emotional needs in early childhood and moving forward. Do your best to breathe and be a calm presence when they are sharing difficult experiences or "emotionally vomiting." Listen deeply, repeat back what you have heard, and offer advice only if it's asked for. End the conversation by asking, "How can I support you?"

* If your children are excited about something and express a strong interest in an activity or new hobby, do what you can to support them in pursuing things that they feel called to do. Even if it doesn't work out the way they planned, it may be a disappointment or experience they require to move to the next stage of development.

* Be curious about your children's points of view and allow them to share, even if they disagree with you. Their ability to practice many different perspectives and options allows them to figure out what is true for them.

* Role model self-care and remind your children that self-care is an important part of their daily experiences. Encourage them to rest, relax, and take breaks. Demonstrate that self-care is an essential part of personal responsibility, that making ourselves a priority is the first step toward health and helping others.

* Talk to your children about the energy they bring into every situation. Explain that they have the power to shift every dynamic by focusing solely on their own words and behavior. Not every outcome will be in their favor, but they are more likely to get their needs met if they pay attention to how they show up.

# THE RIGHT TO LOVE AND BE LOVED

*Loving Ourselves and Others*

Heart center

## GREEN

There is no charm equal to tenderness of heart.

—JANE AUSTEN, *Emma*

## Openheartedness

The heart chakra is where we experience love, warmth, joy, and connection to others. It's the center of our deep bonds, our sense of caring and compassion, and the experience of self-love, generosity, and respect.

Stop reading for a second and point to yourself— notice where you are pointing. I assume you are pointing to your heart, and I doubt any of you are pointing to your heads—yet so many of us live our lives stuck in our minds, believing that's where we reside. The heart center is our essence, the place we are always trying to get back to, the place where we feel in most alignment with ourselves and others.

The "way of the heart" or the "path of the heart" means living from this place of knowing, living a life with loving kindness and compassion toward others. It is where we can experience self-love and inherent worthiness, while maintaining a deep sense of humility.

When people experience pain, they tend to choose one of two paths: protect the heart at all costs by shutting out risky emotional experiences or keep the heart open and accept that love *is* risk. While protecting the heart seems simplest or most logical, it actually creates more pain going forward, keeping us disconnected from ourselves and others, hurting our relationships and our ability to offer and receive love.

The depth of joy and happiness we are able to experience is in direct proportion to the amount of openheartedness we can endure. The best feelings in life come from our willingness to take risks; breakups, death, loss, and betrayal are all possible outcomes of great love. They all began with an openhearted willingness, with an awareness that our greatest joys can lead to our greatest suffering.

Love requires us to risk our hearts, and the more love we offer, the more vulnerable we'll feel. Yet the inability to risk being vulnerable is the beginning of the end for our relationships. Being vulnerable is about being direct and honest about how we feel, by sharing who we are and what we need. While some still associate vulnerability with weakness, vulnerability is actually the ultimate demonstration of strength and bravery, a willingness to offer our true selves rather than a muted or fake version of who we think we're supposed to be.

Even with the most vulnerable and sincere offering of love, none of us is guaranteed love in return. We will inevitably experience loss and heartache; we will be devastated and shocked by what life offers. Devastation and shock can crack the shell that we build around our hearts. The shell was built to make us feel safe, to provide stability and certainty as we move through our lives. But the more pain, the more cracks, the more we are allowed access to what lives underneath.

The cracks are an opportunity to dive deeper into ourselves and pay attention to what we've been trying to repress or avoid. This is how we get back to our true selves and allow our hearts to mature and expand with compassion and resiliency. It's an opportunity to return to how we began, to live from the inside out rather than the outside in, to focus on what matters to us rather than what we were told was most important.

When I was in graduate school to become a social worker, I was told that the first semester of classes was like a "weeding-out process" for students who were only on a mission to heal themselves. The thought was they were in school for the wrong reasons, that focusing on their own self-growth somehow took them away from the essence of social work.

While I'm sure there are a few people who go to school only to focus on themselves and remain stuck in a narcissistic pattern of self-focus and self-diagnosis, I found that the vast majority of my classmates wanted to take their experiences and transcend them into something meaningful and helpful. Their past pain or challenges were not a hindrance to their ability to do social work; it was their superpower.

Part of the social work training was learning more about ourselves and how to process our experiences, but then we were able to use this knowledge to alleviate pain and struggle for other people. I have been teaching social work at a university for the past ten years, and I see the same thing in my students. Many of my students have difficult lives and tough stories, but their experiences drive their desire to be an advocate for others, to ensure that other people don't have to go through what they went through.

I see this in my niece who struggled with learning disabilities and decided to become a special ed teacher. I see this in my friends who chose to become nurses or hospice workers because they deeply appreciated how they or their loved ones were cared for in a crisis. I see this with my friends in recovery who decided to become addiction counselors. I see this in myself as someone who thought being highly sensitive and emotional was a problem, but in actuality it was my greatest gift and now the core of my professional work.

We don't have to run from our pain, and pain doesn't mean we are broken. Instead, it can offer us a place where we can make a difference, an area of expertise that we didn't ask for but are willing to accept in order to help others. Pain wakes us up to who we are and expands our ability to understand ourselves. Then we can offer this authentic service to the world.

We want our kids to grow up to be resilient, compassionate, and strong, but we may hinder their ability to develop these skills by being overprotective or overindulgent. Pain becomes something to avoid rather than something to learn from. We can teach our children to engage with the world from a place of openheartedness, to practice taking risks, and allow them to struggle and learn, to trust that they are built to manage struggle and that their true selves are often revealed by things they would never choose.

When our kids get their hearts broken by a friend, an unsuccessful tryout, a love interest, or any type of rejection, we can allow them to feel it and to sit with them when they are uncomfortable and unmoored. Pain is a metamorphosis, a process of becoming a wiser, more deepened self. They will know it's okay to feel the pain if we can be present for it, if we can listen, support, and give them permission to fall apart and come back together. They will understand this as a necessary part of life if we allow for what's happening, if we don't try to rush their process of healing because of our own discomfort.

## Empathy

Empathy is integral to emotional intelligence and the ability to connect with others. It comes from the German word *Einfühlung*, meaning "feeling in," and just as there are many ways to feel, there are multiple ways to experience empathy. With the heart chakra, balance and awareness are less about focusing on who or what you love and more about examining *how* you love.

Empathy is the ability to step into someone else's shoes to understand their feelings and perspectives. It is different from kindness or pity and different from the Golden Rule, "Do unto others as you would have them do unto you." Empathy is not about offering other people what you need; it's about understanding what they need and offering that instead.

Brené Brown's research describes empathy as the key component in fighting shame, and shame-prone thinking is highly correlated with depression, suicidal ideation, substance use and abuse, and eating disorders. The best way to overcome shame is to talk with people who can respond empathetically. The underlying message from shame is there is something about us that makes us unlovable or undeserving of connection, but if we can talk openly about these fears and receive empathy in return, this narrative is disproved and shame can't survive.

Most people, especially parents, believe they are being empathetic when listening to their kids, but a lack of self-awareness or overall discomfort can push them toward teaching lessons, judgment, or avoidance. Nursing scholar Theresa Wiseman noted four attributes that set the stage for true empathy:

1. **Perspective taking**—Our ability to see the world as others see it requires putting our stuff aside so we can see the situation through someone else's eyes.

2. **Nonjudgment**—Judgment of another person's situation discounts their experience and is usually an attempt to protect us from feeling discomfort.

3. **Recognize emotion**—To understand another person's feelings, we have to understand our own (as we discussed in Chakra Two). We also need to put our feelings aside so we can hear and honor the feelings of another.

4. **Communicate emotion**—Understand and articulate what is being expressed without unnecessary commentary. Instead of playing things down ("It could be worse . . .") or trying to find a silver lining ("At least . . ."), just saying "That sounds difficult; tell me more . . ." or "That sounds like it hurts" conveys listening, presence, and validation.

Many of us were raised in situations where we did not feel heard by our parents, or, even worse, our parents were the people we wanted to keep everything from. When I present to parents, I often ask, "How many of you wish your children were afraid of you?" There are usually a few hands and some quiet laughter (raised hands have decreased over the past ten years), and then someone will inevitably yell out, "*Sometimes* I wish they were afraid of me!"

This is an honest answer, and it stems from our desire to control. Rather than ask again and again, we wish we could tell our kids something only once and have them comply. We wish we could warn them about something and have them listen and trust what we say. This is relatable and understandable, but if our children are afraid of us sometimes, then they are afraid of us.

The vast majority of parents tell me their kids know how much they love them, that their kids know they can talk to them if ever they are in trouble. But I have worked with kids for twenty years, from fifth grade through college, and so many of them do not feel this way. In fact, they often work hard to keep their deepest and darkest fears from their parents.

Parents love their kids, but the internal feeling of love is different from an external practice of being empathetic. In other words, there is a big difference between loving our children and our children feeling loved.

We need to ask ourselves whether we can see our kids' point of view. Do we do our best to put on our kid glasses and experience the world the way they do? Do we listen without judgment and allow them to share their story and challenges without saying, "I told you so" or "If you just would have listened"? Do we understand why they feel the way they do, or do we tell them their feelings aren't valid and that they should feel differently? And can we reflect back what they are saying to demonstrate that we are listening and not turn away because of our own disappointment or discomfort?

If you had empathetic interactions with your parents in childhood, you know how such support and validation lead to trust and connection. If you didn't, which is a lot more typical, it can be more difficult to trust the difference it could have made in the direst situations. The ability to communicate fears and get true reassurance or validation from your parents plays a significant role in the choices and challenges we take on and avoid.

As parents we are given the opportunity every day to practice empathy with our kids, to show up with an awareness of what our kids need in their most difficult moments. When I work with parents who are working on more empathetic responses, I usually tell them to be the person they wish they would have had when they were growing up.

Being an empathetic parent means giving our kids permission to have multiple support systems, to encourage relationships with other trusting adults so our kids have a variety of people they can call when struggling. Some parents get jealous or feel left out when their children confide in other adults, but it's in those moments when it's important to question the big picture. Do we want to be the only person that our kids can trust, or do we want them to develop other strong and trusting relationships so they can feel supported by a village?

When each of my daughters turned thirteen, we had their "13" party to welcome them to their teenage years. I invited family members and friends who loved my girls and asked them to share their experiences of being a teen and what they wished they knew. I also made it clear that all of these women were available if they ever needed support. I clearly stated that while I would always be there for them, my greatest hope is that they knew there was a community of people who were willing to help them and support them.

The perspective-taking part of empathy teaches us that sometimes our kids need older kids or young adults to confide in, that we may not be the best support systems in certain situations because we don't have the information or perspective they need in the moment.

We can also allow our children to be confidants to their friends or family members without trying to get involved. Several times I have asked my daughters about situations with their friends or cousins, and they have respectfully declined to answer my questions. They know the importance of trust and being a confidante, and I admire their ability to be this kind of friend.

I have also told my daughters that if they ever feel scared for a friend or worry about someone's life or health that they should always come to me and I will help. I am encouraged that they have all taken me up on this offer, even though in the moment it felt painful and what to do next felt uncertain. Even so, I continue to remind them that this offer is always on the table, and I won't look away from their pain or the pain of the people they care about. I say it as an open invitation that I will be a calm presence in the scariest of times, and I do what I can to demonstrate this on a daily basis.

Practicing empathy not only strengthens our relationships with our kids, but also teaches our children how to be empathetic with others. This includes how they will respond to us when we are challenged or stressed. During presentations I always point out that yelling at our kids to be kind and considerate is a bit contradictory, and we have to consider practicing what we want them to learn.

We will never do it perfectly—I somehow always end up sharing my own teenage stories when my girls are talking about their lives. I can feel their annoyance when I bust in with my stories about growing up in the eighties, and I realize how unhelpful I am because they are growing up at such a different time. I have no idea what it's like to grow up in the social media age while doing school-shooter drills with climate change as a constant existential threat.

Ironically, today I am writing about empathy and we are in the middle of a pandemic, and people all over the world are isolated in their homes. We are worried about our families, our health-care workers and health-care system, our economy, and what is still yet to come.

When our leaders were encouraging people to stay home, the initial focus was a plea to individuals to stay safe and not get exposed. While some were more worried due to age or health issues, many continued on with their daily lives, unafraid and unwilling to make any big changes.

But the more we heard, the more we realized it was not about our individual needs; it was about the collective whole. Even if a person didn't feel at risk, the idea that we could unknowingly become a spreader and hurt others in the process led to never-before-experienced lifestyle changes.

This perspective dramatically changed the tone of the conversation, and instead of focusing solely on ourselves, we were encouraged to make choices for the common good. This led to some governors closing schools and businesses; this led to food drives and people sewing personal protective equipment for frontline workers. This led to an outpouring of people who were willing to help and support those who were most in need.

Our empathetic responses allowed us to accept something that was unheard of such a short time ago, and our ability to give and support others allowed us to cope with the unimaginable. It's once again a reminder that empathy is not just about feeling love; it's the practice of understanding and showing up in the way that's best for the individual or the whole.

## Self-Compassion

Evolutionary psychologists have explained that we all have a *negativity bias*, an instinct that gives our negative experiences a lot of power. We've evolved to notice our flaws and mistakes more than our successes.

A long time ago our brains evolved with only one function—to survive. We needed anxiety and worry so we could stay vigilant about staying safe and alive, and the most worried and anxious people ran away from anything that looked like a lion so they wouldn't be eaten. The super laid-back person didn't worry enough about the lion, so they didn't survive and neither did their genes.

This means that we are the genetic offspring of very worried yet surviving people, and our brain is programmed similarly. We pay more attention to the negative than the positive, and the "bad" stuff tends to grab our attention, stay in our minds, and influence our decisions.

The problem is that we are no longer running from lions on a daily basis, so we are worried and anxious about things that aren't actually life or death—like being late or what we are wearing or being overly concerned about what others think of us.

These perceived problems dominate our thinking and distract us from what's actually working. Instead of enjoying the good, we remain absorbed by worry and self-criticism, believing that we are doing everything wrong and that there is something inherently wrong with us.

This is good when our safety or moral integrity is on the line because we can learn lessons from our mistakes, but it can be a problem when we forget something on our to-do list or say something embarrassing and then degrade ourselves by launching into a shame spiral.

Such negative stress and self-criticism take a toll on our minds and bodies, leading to ruminating thoughts that can sabotage our daily experience and stimulate inflammation mechanisms that can lead to chronic illness or faster aging. Chronic self-criticism can also lead to symptoms of depression, anxiety, substance abuse, and a negative self-image. We think being hard on ourselves will make us tougher and less "lazy," but studies show that it actually decreases our motivation and productivity and can lead us to being preoccupied with failure.[1]

Self-compassion researcher Kristen Neff explains that when our fight-flight-freeze response is triggered by a threat to our self-concept, we turn on ourselves, making us the attacker and the attacked. We react by self-criticizing (fight), isolating (flight), and ruminating (freeze). Self-compassion literally does the opposite of these stress reactions by instead practicing self-kindness instead of self-criticism, respecting our common humanity instead of isolating, and practicing mindfulness instead of ruminating.

Self-kindness is our ability to treat ourselves as we would a friend, to extend the same generosity to ourselves as we would a loved one. And common humanity is the recognition that we are all in this together, that any emotion or experience has undeniably been felt or shared by another, which means we are never alone.

Mindfulness allows us to notice our thoughts and feelings nonjudgmentally without suppressing or exaggerating them in the moment. We have to pay attention to our pain if we want to have compassion for our pain, and mindfulness allows us to notice our feelings without becoming overidentified with them.

Self-kindness, common humanity, and mindfulness are the key practices to stop the cycle of shame and deactivate the threat-defense system, allowing us to self-regulate in a more healthy and productive way. Things will not always go the way we expected, and we will inevitably encounter frustrations, losses, and mistakes as well as fall short of our expectations. This is the human condition, and the more we are able to open our hearts to this reality instead of fighting against it, the more compassion we will have for ourselves and everyone we encounter.

My generation was raised in the heart of the self-esteem movement, where the focus was on evaluating ourselves positively mostly based on how we compared to others. Self-esteem requires feeling special and above average, yet it's logically impossible for every human to feel above average at the same time. We are deeply offended if someone refers to us as average and are always striving to feel superior, resulting in constant social comparison and an endless game of king of the hill. With this model, it isn't surprising that bullies can actually have high self-esteem because picking on others boosts their self-image and makes them feel more powerful.

In the process of trying to see ourselves as better than others, we also eviscerate ourselves with self-criticism when we don't meet our own standards. As soon as we don't feel bigger or at least comparable to others, which is at some point inevitable, our worthiness plummets. This leaves us vacillating between believing we are better than others or never good enough, mood swings that can lead to insecurity, anxiety, and depression.

Self-compassion is different in that it's not based on positive judgments or evaluations; it's a way of relating to ourselves. It involves being kind to ourselves when we win or lose without being harsh or overly self-critical. It's about recognizing that the human condition is imperfect, allowing us to feel connected to others when we suffer rather than feeling separate or isolated. Rather than suppressing our pain or exaggerating our situation, we practice seeing ourselves and our situations clearly and sending ourselves love instead of pain.

Most important, self-compassion doesn't demand that we see ourselves as better than other people. Self-compassion allows us to stay connected to ourselves and others in the midst of a challenge, rather than feeling unworthy or unlovable when things don't go our way. Kristin Neff's research found that self-compassion offers the same benefits as high self-esteem without the potential downsides such as narcissism, social comparison, or ego defensiveness.

Self-compassion allows us to stay in our heart center and soothe ourselves when life is hard. It's a way to practice self-love instead of self-harm, to offer ourselves support rather than condemnation. If we were raised to beat

ourselves up incessantly or to compare our lives to everyone around us, then our heart center may be accustomed
to feeling attacked. Inflicting self-pain may feel normal-
ized, our minds insisting that it's a necessary form of internal punishment that will lead to our becoming "better."
Self-compassion can feel like a cop-out, like we are being
too soft or letting ourselves off the hook.

If we were taught this and never questioned this behavior, we are inevitably sharing this mentality with our kids.
Instead of soothing their pain, we use threats and fear because we believe it will change their behavior. Instead of
encouraging their ability to get a B+, we question why they
aren't getting an A+. We teach them to beat themselves up
in the name of getting better or stronger, when in reality
we are teaching them how to self-loathe and not feel good
until they are better than everybody else.

This is why it's important to really explore self-
compassion, to find the yin-yang duality that is both passive
and active. The yin aspect of self-compassion is comforting
ourselves in a soothing and validating way, and the yang aspect is focusing on how to protect and motivate ourselves
so we can remain productive and active. Sometimes it's
about soothing ourselves, and sometimes it's about figuring out what we need to protect ourselves. Sometimes it's
about accepting and validating who we are, and sometimes
it's about getting up and doing something active to stay
motivated. Self-compassion is not about letting ourselves
off the hook; it's about taking responsibility for the way we

treat ourselves and others. The common thread is a caring attitude and proceeding with a maturity about what caring looks like.

Self-compassion doesn't mean that we aren't learning from our challenges or pain; in fact, practicing self-compassion makes it more likely that we are able to learn from experiences because our minds and hearts stay open to our experiences. We are able to see and own what's happening with less defensiveness and anger, allowing us to respond to ourselves and others appropriately.

Self-compassion is about cultivating a more constructive response to difficult times, where instead of deciding we are horrible or attempting to massage our ego by telling ourselves we are always awesome, we simply accept our results for what they are and see them as inevitable learning experiences.

The research has demonstrated that self-compassion increases our "growth mindset," the belief that abilities develop through understanding, dedication, and hard work. Self-compassion increases our motivation to confront our challenges and take steps to do better (instead of being incessantly self-flagellating). It also gets us through our down-and-out stages more quickly so we can get back to work and find new paths toward success.

**Self-compassion is not a cop-out, and it's the opposite of being complacent or lazy. Practicing self-compassion allows us to be more resilient and motivated in the face of setbacks so we can continue on even in the face of failure, leading to a better relationship with ourselves and our kids.**

## Breathing

The fourth chakra focuses on the emotions of love and compassion, and it physically focuses on the heart and the lungs, making breathing a vital component in our ability to keep our hearts open. Breathing is our life force, whether we participate in it or just turn it over to our autonomic nervous system. Even without paying attention, our body knows how to breathe. We don't have to think about it; it just happens by the fact of our existence.

But the natural rhythm of breathing can be challenged for a number of reasons, sometimes to the point where it's difficult to breathe at all (think panic attacks). A shallower version of breathing may have become habitual over time, or certain life events unconsciously trigger an adaptive breathing response, where the breathing becomes rapid and shallow or maybe even unknowingly held for a certain period of time.

Whether we are aware of these reactions or not, they most likely have a memory in your body, often triggered by early traumatic experiences. Even if you can't remember details, the body remembers, and it responds to the feelings, smells, sights, and sounds with a retained way of breathing.

When I was young, I often struggled to get a good breath. I would talk about this a lot and even hyperventilate myself trying to pull a good breath through. My physical health seemed fine; at least I didn't have asthma or any other obvious physical limitation. In retrospect, it seems like my inability to deep breathe was connected to my inability to process how I was feeling. I had my own challenges, and my sensitivity and ability to feel other people's emotions weren't yet clear to me. I just felt surrounded by scary feelings, and I didn't know how to carry or express them. This inhibited my breathing, and it made me tired.

This discomfort followed me into adulthood, and in my early thirties I started doing yoga. After a few years of practice, I decided that I needed to become a teacher. Explaining this expensive decision to my husband was difficult, especially when I told him I was indifferent to whether I ever taught my own classes; I just wanted to learn *how* to teach. I eventually realized, and was able to explain, that I wanted to learn how to teach because I wanted to learn how to breathe. I wanted to expand and deepen my practice by learning how to breathe in unison with what I was feeling.

I trained for a year and did become a part-time yoga teacher, but this was short-lived. What I actually became was an engaged and daily student, one who could use breath to move my emotions. When doing a pose or sequence that is challenging, the initial reaction is fear, rejection, or aversion, but yoga is a training ground for learning about managing obstacles. There are poses I loathe, but I can breathe through them, learn how to align better, and notice how I always have the option to move through difficult things with less rejection and more ease.

This gets taken off the mat, where we learn to not run away from fears or challenges but also not to blindly bulldoze our way through them. Yoga is an obvious life metaphor—it's the practice of breathing to stay present while offering ourselves grace in the midst of discomfort. It's about detaching from results and focusing more on the surrender and satisfaction within the process.

There is no mastery of this; I have been doing yoga now for almost twenty years, and I still lapse into fear and get lost in stress. But my lag time is better, and my ability to notice what I'm doing and then start breathing has gotten incrementally better. I am more responsive and less reactive, and, most important, I accept my feelings, even when I don't like them.

The breath is like a barometer for how we're feeling, and it's also a tool. Breathing techniques allow us to shift gears and alter our emotional state because they gently calm the central nervous system. There are many different breathing practices in yoga, and depending on your personality and obstacles, certain ones will speak to you more than others. The following are my three favorite breathing practices, the ones that I use on a daily basis.

The first is just a deep breath in through the nose and a deep breath out through the nose. There is no special skill here; there is no trick. The key is *when* to use it— before speaking to your kids or partner, before yelling at a coworker, before speeding because you are late, and before sending that email. One breath in and then out is a pause. It offers the ability to respond instead of react, to calm the body before making the next choice

I use this every day, all day long. When I'm talking with my daughters, when I'm teaching, when I'm writing, when I'm trying to figure out what to do next, I stop and breathe and then stop and breathe again. It's my brake pedal, and when I use it I have much fewer messes to clean up.

The second type of breathing is often referred to as four-seven-eight breath and was made famous by Dr. Andrew Weil. I use it if I'm having a hard time falling asleep, if I've been sad or angry for an extended period of time, or if I am unsure of what I'm feeling but am just having a hard time pulling a breath through. To me this breathing technique feels like an exercise for the lungs; it's how I expand my rib cage and keep my heart open.

* Start by exhaling any air you are holding and relax your shoulders.

* Close your mouth and inhale silently through your nose as you count to four in your head.

* Then, for seven seconds, hold your breath.

* Then exhale out your mouth for eight seconds (you will make a whooshing sound).

Practice this pattern for four full breaths. It's recommended that four-seven-eight breathing is done for only four cycles when first starting out, and then gradually work up to eight full cycles. It's also recommended to not use this technique unless fully prepared to relax (meaning, don't do this while driving). While it doesn't necessarily have to be used for falling asleep, it can still create a state of deep relaxation.

I've shared this with my daughters when they are having difficulty falling asleep, and I use it when I find myself using the words *stressed* or *busy* too many times in one day. It's centering and allows me to expand and then release what I no longer need.

The last breathing technique took me a while to accept, but only because I didn't understand its impact. It's called Tonglen, the Tibetan practice of "sending and receiving." *Tong* means "sending out" or "letting go," and *-len* means "receiving" or "accepting." It's practiced by breathing in the bad and breathing out the good, a choice to breathe in the suffering of all sentient beings.

At first I wanted to stay as far away from Tonglen as possible. Because I absorb other people's energies and emotions easily, I thought this would be a practice of taking on what other people are unwilling to feel—therefore doing their work for them. But it's not about absorbing other people's energy; it's about acknowledging the pain of the world.

When the pandemic became a reality, all I could feel on an everyday basis was my own fear and the fear of those around me. It didn't feel like something I could run from, and I needed a way to just allow the fear and pain to be there while staying strong for myself and others. One morning I was so overwhelmed by the news, I decided to try Tonglen. I breathed in the fear I was feeling, and all I breathed out were self-compassion and nonjudgment. Then I breathed in while visualizing the words, pictures, people, problems, all of the pain around me—not as a problem to solve, but as the truth of the moment. And when I breathed out, it felt like an act of love. Breathing in what was happening didn't weigh me down; it opened me up. It felt like I was ingesting the truth of my feelings and the truth of the moment, but then exhaling Truth with a capital *T*.

I started breathing in when I read about health-care workers or people who were really sick. I breathed in their suffering, and I breathed out love and compassion. It felt like an acceptance of the moment, an ability to look squarely at what was happening. By doing this, I could do the next right thing instead of pushing feelings away or pulling the blanket over my head. So much of our pain comes from suppression, an unwillingness to look at or feel what's happening. This is denial, and it steals our energy. Tonglen is the practice of nondenial, the acknowledgment that the other side of pain and fear is care and compassion.

You can do Tonglen for the little girl who is crying at the grocery store and for her tired and angry mother who is yelling at her. You can send out a general sense of relaxation and openness or something specific, like a hug or a kind word or whatever feels right to you at the moment.

It's not all that conceptual; it's almost spontaneous. When you experience a painful situation in this way and stay with it, you can open up your heart and become a source of compassion.

Tonglen can be used on the spot when strong emotions come up unexpectedly, like when you have a painful argument with your spouse or your boss at work and you don't know how to react. You can breathe in the painful feelings and send out a sense of spaciousness and relaxation with the out breath—for yourself, for the person who is angry, and for all the other people who are dealing with a similarly difficult situation. It's an act of compassion for yourself and everyone around you; it's a practice in keeping your heart open in the most challenging of circumstances.

## Grief

Grief is our response to any kind of loss, and while loss is inevitable, the vast majority of people have a deep discomfort with the process of grief. And it is indeed a process, an experience rather than just a feeling. And while grief looks and feels different depending on who you are, too many of us are judged for our experience and often told we are doing it wrong. If we cry and talk about it too much, we are told we need to move on, and if we have the audacity to move forward and find happiness, we are cold and heartless. There is not a lot of room for error in that middle space.

I remember the day that comedian Patton Oswalt announced his relationship with his now wife, Meredith Salenger, a year after his wife died. While there were some well-wishers, many were angry and appalled, deciding that he had "gotten over" his wife too quickly. This is just an example of a million stories, of the many ways we displace our discomfort with grief on other people. What we don't understand about grief is that we never get *over* it; we find a way through it and then a way to manage it. As grief author Nora McInerny says, "You do not move on from this. You move forward with this as just a part of who you are in your DNA."[2]

My clients have described grief as heightened anxiety, and they've been surprised how it can feel like deep-seated fear. Some have described grief as their path to what's true and as a finger-pointing to what matters most. Grief is like a flashlight shining a light on what's necessary, how to survive, and what we need to cope.

My personal experience has contained all of these realizations and more. Grief feels all over the place because it's an individual journey of internal reorganization. Our bodies and minds are working to integrate something painful or unimaginable, and throughout the process we experience ourselves rejecting, shifting, accepting— moving through the discomfort of integrating something that was previously unimaginable. Grief can make life feel meaningless and meaningful at the very same time, and vacillating between the two can feel both scary and enlivening.

Grief literature is often unhelpful because it's loaded with well-meaning but misinformed ideas about what grief feels like. Even the *Diagnostic and Statistical Manual of Mental Disorders* (*DSM-5*), the diagnostic statistical tool that all therapists use for treatment, can point to grieving as a troubling diagnosis rather than a standard sign of coping. This is a controversial topic, and both sides have their own perspective and research, but it's always been concerning to me that professionally some look at grief as a problem to solve rather than the actual solution to the problem.

In traditional Chinese medicine, grief and sadness directly affect the lungs. Every time we breathe in, we absorb oxygen (pure Qi) into our body, before breathing out what we don't need, carbon dioxide. Plants are our most important companions because they are able to reverse that process, absorbing carbon dioxide to transform it into oxygen. This is another demonstration of why breathing is so essential to the heart chakra.

According to the ancient medical texts, when the lung energy is in harmony, we are able to breathe in fresh new ideas and absorb new experiences, as well as being able to breathe out and expel old prejudices and assumptions. Unfortunately, the lungs are directly affected by emotions of sadness and grief, which constrain the organ's feelings and restrict their movement. Being unable to express emotions or being overwhelmed by them can make the lungs feel weak.

About six months after my dad passed away, I got a respiratory flu that my children had before me. They spent about four to five days in bed, but I ended up sick for almost a full month. My fever lasted almost seven days on and off, and once I was through that phase, it was all fatigue, discomfort, and emotion. I was coughing and crying; I had panic attacks and difficulty sleeping at night. I could barely walk down the stairs and could be with people for only short periods of time. I felt ravaged by this illness, as if it was pulling everything I had ever felt up and out. I had to work hard to get better—forcing myself to move and talk instead of isolating.

I gradually got better, and with hindsight it felt like much more than a bad flu—it felt like an opportunity for my body to release seventeen years of grieving my dad's chronic illness. It was an unrelenting experience of worry, caregiving, and fear that "ended" when he died, but it still lived in my body. The physical illness became an opportunity for my lungs to release and move through what was no longer needed.

What I appreciate about this understanding of lungs and emotions in Chinese medicine is that grief is considered pathological only if it is unexpressed or repressed, a reminder that allowing ourselves to feel and grieve is the way we keep ourselves healthy and in balance.

Elisabeth Kübler-Ross was a grief expert who was best known for her five stages of grief: denial (I can't believe this happened), anger (this shouldn't have happened), bargaining (all the what-ifs and regrets), depression (the sadness), and then acceptance (acknowledging the reality). I have read that Kübler-Ross was dismayed that all of her lifelong work around grief was condensed to these stages and that they were often used to organize messy emotions into neat packages. As a grief expert she understood that stages may help identify reactions to loss, but there is no typical response to loss and no typical loss.

Grief researcher David Kessler worked closely with Elisabeth Kübler-Ross (she passed away in 2004), and he was given permission to add a sixth stage, *meaning*, to her stages of grief. He explains that meaning helps us connect to something beyond the loss, and while we connect grief to pain, grief is also a demonstration of love, and in the end the hope is that love is felt and remembered.

We grieve only what we have loved, and this is why it can be difficult to keep our hearts open after experiencing loss. While in deep grief over my first miscarriage, I remember telling my husband that I would prefer a life of numbness over a life of such deep feeling. I have felt that desire for numbness again and again, every time I have lost something or someone I needed. But I, and the vast majority of people I know, return to love even while knowing and experiencing the risks. We love because it makes us who we are, and we grieve when we lose a part of who we are. Grief and love are equally transformative.

If we have grieved well, if we have known the pitfalls, the challenges, and the light, then it is easier to sit with people who are grieving. When our partner loses a job, or when our children experience their first heartbreak, we see and feel the familiar patterns of loss; we recognize the road they are on. But if we have spent our lives avoiding grief, or trying not to feel our disappointment and pain, then the pain of others, especially people we love, can make us deeply uncomfortable, so much so that we may actively negate or shame them for not jumping over their grief the same way we did.

In this situation we have to show compassion to ourselves, to remember that we may have been taught to avoid grief and we are just passing on what we learned. Many of my clients grew up in families that never talked about loved ones after they died and were never told why their parents were divorcing or why the family needed to abruptly move. They were forced to just hold the pain and sit in the uncertainty.

Some were even told to buck up, get over it, not be selfish, or anything to silence them about expressing the pain of loss. This is a vicious and repetitive pattern in families that can be broken in our generation. We get to hold the space for our children to feel their pain instead of suppress it, we get to trust that we have the capacity to manage the ever-changing emotions of the grief process, and we get to know that grieving is what takes us deeper into ourselves. Grief can feel like a breaking heart, but the actual grieving process is about putting the heart back together.

In Japanese philosophy there is something called *wabi-sabi*, which values simplicity and authenticity—an acceptance of the old, the worn, and the asymmetrical. *Wabi-sabi* focuses on the three qualities of life—everything is impermanent, imperfect, and incomplete—and it embraces the understanding that nothing is finished, nothing is perfect, and life rarely works out the way we had planned.

*Wabi-sabi* is where the Japanese practice of *kintsugi* or *kintsukuroi* comes from, an art form that highlights and enhances breaks and cracks to enhance the value of an object. It uses precious metal to bring broken pieces together while enhancing the breaks. Every repaired piece is unique because of the randomness with which they shatter and beautiful way they are put back together.

There is something magical about this art and how it transforms something broken or imperfect and makes it more beautiful—it becomes its own work of art. *Kintsugi* celebrates this process and even makes it the focal point—an acceptance that brokenness is unavoidable but that our brokenness is what creates our depth and beauty.

## *For You*

* Understand that empathy is not about feeling love; it's about how we understand each other and relate to each other's experiences.

* When your kids talk, listen without judgment and allow them share without constantly trying to teach or say, "I told you so."

* Remember that self-compassion is not indulgent; it's the ability to be present with what is happening

and trust that you have the capacity to offer yourself love and understanding.

* Use breathing to slow yourself down and be mindful. Notice how it can reduce or soften negative thinking and keep you present.

* Know that grieving is a healthy and natural process that allows us to take our brokenheartedness and transform it into something beautiful. Allow yourself to cry, and know that difficult times are part of the healing process.

### For Your Kids

* Allow your kids to feel their pain and sit with them while they feel it.

* When your kids tell you a story, put on your kid glasses and look at life the way they do. Relate to their experience and validate their experience.

* Allow your kids to have other adults that they trust and relate to—give them permission to share with other trusted adults so they feel surrounded by a village.

* Teach your kids to be self-compassionate by reminding them they will be more productive and
  have greater brain power if they treat themselves
  kindly, stay present, and remember they are never
  alone.

* Teach your kids how to breathe effectively so they
  can use their physicality to move through difficult
  emotions.

* Allow your kids to grieve and understand that it
  might feel messy, but that messy is a path toward
  growth and change.

.........................

# THE RIGHT TO SPEAK AND HEAR TRUTH

*Valuing Authentic Communication*

Throat

**BLUE**

Tell the truth to yourself first, and to the children.

—MAYA ANGELOU, *interview*,
George Stroumboulopoulos Tonight, *December 31, 2013*

## Self-Expression

The fifth chakra, or throat chakra, is associated with self-expression and communication. It's the ability to speak honestly, receive and process information, and speak with authenticity and truth.

This is where our insides are shared with the outside world, an opportunity to offer what only we have felt and experienced. This makes it a place of deep vulnerability because we fear that what we share may be threatening, uncomfortable, or not enough for others. Speaking what we know may risk our sense of belonging or damage our connections. Our need to be accepted and acceptable can turn our fifth chakra into a bottleneck, stifling who we are and what we know in an effort to be loved and valued.

If the lower chakras are in good order—our need for safety, emotional expression, self-individuation, and compassion—then it's more likely that we can share our own personal truths. But if the lower-chakra aspects of ourselves have been denied or repressed, then we may not even know how to share what we need. We may not have the words or understanding to speak what we are feeling.

In early development we may have shared ourselves and been told to quiet down or that we were being disloyal or disrespectful. We may have been told by society that children are to be seen and not heard or that boys don't cry and girls don't get angry. We may have been taught through a multitude of experiences and events that sharing what we really think and feel is unsafe and that it's best to either stay quiet or join the chorus around us.

Then, when we are adults and in relationships with others, we find it difficult to share who we are or express what we feel. When we are being asked our opinion at work or socially, we pass on the chance, fearing we are wrong and that we will be shamed or ridiculed. Or when we are given the opportunity to share our intimate feelings for another, we are terrified of rejection. These adult experiences are opportunities to reconsider what we learned in childhood, to begin the work of trusting our abilities to use our voices and handle how they are received with a sense of empowerment and humility.

Honest communication reveals what's going on inside of us, and if we were previously traumatized by rage, physical or sexual abuse, or criticism and humiliation, we were taught to live in fear of this kind of exposure. We learned to stay quiet to stay safe, to protect ourselves by never sharing what we feel.

Traumatic experiences have a way of morphing into shame, and shame tells us that what lives inside of us is flawed and that we need to hide it. Our inner voice is our greatest critic, telling us that nobody wants to hear our opinion and that offering ourselves is to risk humiliation and harm. It's a vicious cycle of needing to share to release the shame but being too ashamed to share anything we feel.

The path to change is to practice speaking, ideally with a partner or friend who has demonstrated a willingness to listen. But it could also be a therapist, coach, or parent-type figure, anyone who can hear without judgment and offer compassion instead of criticism.

You can begin with simple things, like favorite movies or favorite books, and then move into other areas that might feel more vulnerable—stories from childhood, fears about the future, or experiences with anxiety and depression. The more we are able to share and feel accepted, the more we will realize that the voice in our head telling us to stay quiet has been self-harming and betraying what is in our best interest.

The more we share, the more we realize our common humanity and how anything we have felt, experienced, or said has been experienced by others. Speaking what we feel and believe is like working a muscle, and the more we utilize the muscle, the stronger it gets. Sharing what we feel inside makes us lighter because we no longer carry the weight of unexpressed feelings or ideas. We free ourselves by speaking what we know and support others by relating to what they feel.

## The Art of Communication

The fifth chakra is also related to our ability to effectively communicate, specifically how to practice and develop authentic and connective communication. Authentic communication does not come easily; there's a delicate balance between saying what we mean while staying tactful and diplomatic.

When I talk to fifth grade girls about sharing their feelings, they initially believe this gives them permission to say anything that comes to mind, even hurtful things directed at specific people. This is when we discuss the difference between content and context, that it's not just about what you feel, but you also need to consider why you are feeling it, why you are sharing it, how you will express it, and what it will accomplish. *It's not what you say; it's how you say it and why.*

Effective communication is a dance with many moving parts. What we feel and want to say is important, but how we deliver what we want to say is *more* important. The sound of our voice and our body language play a role in how everything is received. That's why communication is an ongoing practice, because every experience offers us either what feels like successful connection or an opportunity to consider how we could have been more thoughtful with our words or ability to listen.

Parents often ask how they should talk to their kids or ask for specific words they should say. It can be a good idea to be coached in what's most effective, but it's less about the right words and more about what's behind the words. The way we feel comes across in how we sound, and our sincerity comes across in our energy and body language. Having an effective conversation is less about word choice and more about the energy behind our words. Listeners are more attuned to how they feel during the conversation rather than remembering the specific words that are spoken.

How are you making your kids feel while you talk to them, and why are you sharing what you are sharing? Are you offering something that might be helpful, or is your intention to convince and manipulate behavior? While there can be a fine line when considering this question, whatever the intent it can usually be felt by the person listening. Kids know when their parents are trying to "convince" them to do something, and fifth graders know when a friend is saying something to be hurtful rather than helpful.

Your intention may be focused around helping, but that doesn't matter if your children are no longer listening because they feel under attack. It's just as important, if not more important, to pay attention to the energy we are carrying when speaking. We may be having a tough day because of work, and then we yell at our kids about their toys being all over the floor. We may feel insecure about how we are perceived, so we tell our kids to act or look a certain way so we feel better about ourselves. It doesn't matter what words we choose, children can feel this inauthenticity, and it's usually why they push back. They know it's yours and not really about them, so they question why they have become the receiver of your pain and discomfort.

We also have to be thoughtful about the words we choose and how they will be understood. When my daughters were young and would take something that wasn't theirs, I would say, "You can't take that." This made no sense to them, because they *did* just take it and had already demonstrated they could. I had to learn to be thoughtful and creative in how I talked to my girls, to point out what they did and then explain why they may *be able* to take something, but it's not a good choice.

We don't have permission to dump everything we think and feel on top of people and then believe we can maintain a healthy relationship. Saying something unkind and then saying it was a joke or that the other person is too sensitive is irresponsible and mean, and telling our kids or partners how to think and act or yelling at them for not thinking and acting the way we would is unfair and will eventually harm the relationship.

We may feel righteous about what we say and why we say it, believing that others pushed us to do or say whatever we've just expressed. It is human to be emotional and get caught up in the moment, but it's unfair to blame others for what you are saying or how you are saying it. Blaming others is common in adolescence when kids are developing a self-identity and figuring out how to communicate, but it's also common for physical and emotional abusers, because they don't take any responsibility for their actions, blaming their victim as the person who incited the violence.

These are the extremes, and most of us fall somewhere in between. We may occasionally lose control through yelling or word choice, but instead of shifting blame we can view it as a wake-up call to pay attention to the underlying pain behind the yelling. It may be a pattern from childhood or more recent worries that we are trying to suppress. But either way, we can take responsibility for the content and context of our communication.

This is very true in partnership, and healthy communication with a partner can be a foundational training ground for healthy communication in parenting. Healthy communication with friends and family is also foundational and a great place to practice, but if healthy partner communication is demonstrated in the home, then children can learn through role modeling as well as their interactions with us.

When I want to share something difficult with my husband, I make it a priority and find a good time. Asking for an impromptu big talk at the beginning of the World Series feels inconsiderate and ineffective, but I also don't want to plan so far ahead that we both worry about our "big talk" all day. Ideally, there are date nights, walks, or scheduled opportunities for connection, so talks are naturally built into our lives. But whatever the plan, the goal is to approach it calmly.

I start by taking responsibility for my part. Maybe I haven't been clear about my needs, or maybe I've been quiet or suppressing my annoyance for a long time and could have spoken up earlier. Taking responsibility for my part lends to a feeling of openness and vulnerability in the discussion, an ability to express disappointment or disagreement, but an honesty about how we both contributed to the existing problem.

It's easier to listen when the person across from you has already recognized their role in a situation. Just saying we are overwhelmed or stressed is too general and doesn't offer an opportunity for real understanding or change. We need to be clear and honest about our difficult feelings, to share that we feel angry, disappointed, abandoned, or lonely—the more defined our feeling, the easier it will be to discuss and manage.

Yelling, hitting, storming out, or slamming doors may relay the same type of feelings, but expressing anything violently will keep it from being heard. Reacting physically or in an emotionally scary way automatically puts the other person, whether it's your partner or your child, on the defensive. When we are defensive, we shut down and are unable to hear. We go into survival mode rather than being open to introspection or connection.

Again, these more destructive patterns may have been role modeled for you as a child, or maybe you have had previous relationships that played out this way. But a healthy relationship necessitates an ability to have safe conversation, to deliver feelings and needs without fear or force, so the person in front of us can reciprocate similarly.

It's a contradictory message to yell at our kids that they need to be kind or shame them into giving from the heart. We can suggest and encourage, but the strongest possibility that they will act or react in a certain way is through our role modeling and supportive interactions with them on a daily basis.

If we slam doors or stomp out, that's what our kids will learn to do. If we suppress all of our feelings or unleash all of our feelings on the family, that is how they will manage their emotions. They learn through watching, and they learn through their interactions with us.

The practice of communicating calmly and effectively can be one step forward, two steps back. We not only need to be thoughtful about our own emotional state and intention, but also need to be thoughtful about the person in front of us, how they best receive information, and what we can consider from their point of view.

Things will not always flow perfectly, but even the imperfect conversations are opportunities to recognize how we could have expressed or received something more effectively. When it comes to communication, our previous chakras play vital roles: our sense of safety (chakra one), our ability to regulate our emotions (chakra two), our sense of self (chakra three), and our ability to be empathetic and compassionate (chakra four) are the keys to effective communication. Being triggered in any one of these areas can throw off our ability to own our behavior and consider the needs of another.

That is why this area of development may highlight the need to focus on another area of development. We may recognize through our communication that we always feel unsafe and that we need to go back and focus on our sense of grounding and stability. Or we may recognize that we don't know what we want or what we would even ask for, and we have to go back to our sense of self and figure out how to tap into our own needs.

How we communicate is an indicator of how we are managing all the pieces of ourselves, and poor communication is an opportunity to notice what's lacking and, if possible, pay attention to the aspects of ourselves that need the most support and compassion.

In that way, communication becomes an effective recalibration tool, a way of recognizing what's going on in ourselves at all times. It also forces us to pay attention to the needs of others rather than focusing solely on what we need to share.

## Words Are Things

In Don Miguel Ruiz's book *The Four Agreements*, the first agreement is *Be Impeccable with Your Word*, meaning our lives become more manageable if we speak with integrity and honesty and avoid speaking negatively about ourselves and others. His challenge is to use our words to inspire truth and love.

The first agreement is a reminder to notice our words and why we say them and to become more thoughtful about our word choices. Maya Angelou explained the importance of this when she said, "Words are things. . . . [S]omeday we'll be able to measure the power of words. I think they are things. They get on the walls. They get in your wallpaper. They get in your rugs, in your upholstery, and your clothes, and finally into you."[1]

Words have the power to transform our thinking, for better or worse, influencing our choices and beliefs about ourselves and others. If our words are thoughtless, painful, or harmful, they can cause mass destruction.

Understanding the power of words motivates us to use them conscientiously, to not be flippant or insensitive. We have the freedom to choose what we say, but freedom necessitates responsibility and a willingness to recognize the consequences of our choices.

Our intentions may be good, but if the words we choose create a negative impact, then our good intentions aren't enough. Words can mean different things depending upon the receiver, and if the receiver feels disrespected or hurt after absorbing what was said, it's an opportunity for listening and understanding. The belief that we shouldn't have to consider our word choices is the belief that our perspective is the only correct one and that other people's life experiences should be minimized or aren't as valuable.

We are always growing and learning; this ability never goes away, no matter how old or experienced we are. The ability to become more aware of how we impact the people around us is how we stretch; it's an opportunity to expand our awareness and listen to other people's lived experience. It's our responsibility to become more knowledgeable about the perspective of others and develop our communication so we are contributing to well-being rather than doing harm.

This is especially true with our children. If we offer our unsolicited advice about everything they do, or we comment on what we think they should be doing, then our kids will eventually take offense. We can be righteous and decide they have no right to be offended, but as we stay stuck in our story, they disconnect from us and the relationship suffers.

If our children tell us that our words hurt them, it's an invitation to be creative about how we communicate. What we have done in the past or what we are doing right now isn't working, so we may need to find new ways to talk. When my oldest was little, she told me that she didn't like telling me difficult things because I appeared disappointed when I listened and sounded disappointed when I talked. I wanted to argue the fact that I was *not* disappointed, but she was sharing her experience so I decided to listen and get creative.

We decided that when she wanted to tell me something difficult, she would write to me in a notebook and leave it on my bed. I would write back, and then, if necessary, we would continue to discuss it face-to-face. She felt more comfortable discussing it once the difficult things had been written and read, because then my face didn't give away so many feelings.

We have continued to use this method throughout her life, and she has shared some of her most difficult moments with me in writing. I found that this was helpful for both of us because I was able to thoughtfully consider a response, keeping our communication healthy and respectful. My daughter has also used writing to share her gratitude and love, writing me lovely cards on the important holidays.

With all my daughters, I have found that text messages, Post-it notes on their doors, or even Snapchat posts have been effective ways to communicate our love and challenges. With my college students, I have found that some prefer face-to-face discussions, and some prefer long emails. Instead of insisting on one way to communicate, I insist on finding the most helpful and supportive way to communicate. This has created trusting relationships with people I care about, where what we say and how we say it can both be considered.

## Heard and Understood

As a clinician, I know that what my clients need most is to be heard and understood. Listening and acknowledging their perspectives is the first step in helping them move forward in a healthy way. This is true for all human beings, and this is definitely true for our children. Not only do our children want to be known, but they especially want to be known by their parents. They want to feel seen and safe, and they want to feel free and be accepted.

Our ability to be active listeners is how our children will feel known in our presence. Effective communication is not about perfect words or the ideal debate; it's about the practice of listening intently, of demonstrating an undivided attention that makes the person who is speaking feel valued.

Most of the time we aren't really listening; we are just waiting for an opening to make our point, leading to inadequate communication and misunderstandings in our most important relationships. Our brain is in such a hurry to move to the next thing or check the next box on our list, we forget what's most important—we forget to pay attention.

Being heard is one of the most profound human needs, and when met by an attentive listener, intimacy and safety are created. Healing takes place when our story, feelings, or opinions are heard and understood, even if it doesn't change the experience we are having or the behavior of others. Being heard is not always about finding solutions; it's about being recognized and having our truth validated, which honors our existence and perspective.

When we are heard and understood, we begin to believe that we matter. Knowing that we matter sets the tone for our lives, guiding our choices and our ability to have a sense of self. All parents want this for their children, but the practice of listening can feel daunting, especially if this kind of communication has never been role modeled or if we believe that our role is to solve problems rather than be an attentive listener.

We jump to problem solving when we are trying to decrease our discomfort about how our children are feeling and ultimately how they are making us feel in the moment. If we believe that it's our job to keep our kids from feeling pain or challenge, then we try to talk them out of their pain and explain away what they share. But it's not our job to keep our kids from feeling pain and discomfort; in fact, it's our work to allow them to feel whatever they feel and support them as they work through it.

Supporting them while they work through it means listening and allowing, understanding and comforting. If our kids ask for feedback or help, then the door is open to share, but most of the time they just need to know that we get it. They need a space to feel safe and known; they need to know that no matter what they feel or experience, they still safely belong.

What people fear most is being an outcast, not feeling accepted, or not belonging. This is an understandable evolutionary fear based in needing community to survive. Big feelings, mistakes, and challenges feel like they can threaten our sense of security and may lead us to being rejected and unloved. Underneath all the angry words and defensiveness, there is the fear that we aren't enough.

Being an active listener requires our ability to relax, pay attention to the person in front of us, and actually contemplate what they are trying to say. Active listening can actually slow down the pace of the person talking to us, because the pressure to be understood decreases when someone is really listening. When communicating, we reciprocate what we are experiencing, so if the person across from us is calm, it's easier for us to be calm.

This is difficult when we are dealing with a child or teen who is feeling out of control, because our autopilot response will be to react similarly. This is why we need to breathe and pay attention, to get back to active listening and realize that the person in front of us may seem combative but they are also releasing a lot of feelings that are healthy to release. Our ability to stay calm when the person across from us can't leads to safer and more effective communication.

As a parent it can feel unfair that we are being asked to do all of this difficult work, to stay calm in the midst of difficult communication, to pay attention when no one is paying attention to us. That's why self-awareness and self-care are an essential part of parenting. It can feel almost impossible to help someone know they belong if we don't feel like we belong, and it feels difficult to not get defensive if no one has ever considered our point of view.

Parenting opens up parts of us we thought we had put away for good. It brings back our positive memories, but also the parts of childhood that we would rather not revisit. I smoked a cigarette for the first time when I was twelve and had my first drink the same year, and some of my good friends were already sexually active. I had to reconcile these experiences when my own daughter turned twelve, because looking at her made it seem impossible that I was only her age when experiencing so many adult things.

In my mind, I had made myself so much older or aware, almost like a protection that my choices or experiences were somehow mature or typical. I have heard similar things from my clients who were molested or had sexual experiences with older partners when they were actually quite young. They now see themselves more clearly when they look at their children, and feelings of grief come up as they realize that they were taken advantage of or simply did not have the maturity to handle what was happening.

These experiences are painful, but they are also cathartic. Having a child did not create these feelings; they had been living inside of us without a way to be heard or understood. Having a child is an opportunity to account for every aspect of our lives and our way of being. It's an opportunity to acknowledge what we didn't have the words for when we were young and forgive ourselves for what we didn't have the ability to understand.

Another common theme of my clients is their awareness that they were the child of an alcoholic or addict. While some kids grow up acknowledging family addiction and understanding the ramifications, others grow up in more of a denial state, creating stories or excuses in childhood to buffer the chaos or challenges in their home environment. But when they become parents, there is greater clarity that the chaos they tried to manage or deny was due to a family member struggling with addiction.

This realization can be painful, but it's important to understand that the pain is not new; it's always been true and can now be seen with mature eyes. Seeing what was true can lessen the guilt for past mistakes or misunderstandings, allowing us to reflect on our childhoods with greater understanding and compassion. When something is too heavy or burdensome for a child to hold, the brain does its best to create a story or way of thinking that makes it more manageable. The hope is that once we have more maturity and access to support, we can reconcile what we may have been unable to acknowledge so we can honor the truth and soothe the child within us. An unwillingness to do this can cause us to repeat instead of repair patterns and possibly perpetuate the same cycle of dysfunction in our own family.

The realizations about our past come fast and furious when we become parents, and while it can feel like something to run from, our willingness to feel and accept is the way through. Our ability to acknowledge what we have experienced and move forward with self-compassion is what allows us to be present for ourselves and our children.

## Learning Differences

When I was studying to become a teacher, one of my greatest lessons was that students have different ways of learning. Some are auditory, some are more visual, some are more kinesthetic (hands-on), and some are a mix of all three, opening my eyes to the fact that a one-size-fits-all learning style is not sufficient.

I am somewhat evenly a visual and auditory learner, with kinesthetic much farther down the list, so hands-on group work has always felt like a chore. I always felt bad about this because the people around me always seemed to thrive in group work, but to me it felt like going through the motions. Instead of shaming myself for not enjoying group projects or believing that group projects were inherently bad or unnecessary, I began to pay attention to my best learning style and make room for the way others became educated.

We tend to undervalue skill sets that aren't as emphasized in the school system but are still necessary for our society to function, causing us to take paths or go into careers that don't fit our skills or interests.

As a kid who was much more existential and interpersonal, I didn't think of myself as "smart" in traditional school situations where a more logical-mathematical approach was valued. I had to work much harder to achieve what others so easily mastered, and my innate ability to understand people and be curious about the world was never noticed as a skill for my future success. But once I was done with traditional education, my more innate skills were able to take over and lead the way in my master's program and my eventual career as a therapist. If we are able to respect and notice our children's native genius, we may be less worried about straight As and more focused on curiosity and enhancing what comes easily and naturally.

This is similar to why a personality test can be interesting in helping us understand ourselves and others. I remember taking my first personality test (the DiSC, which stands for four behavioral traits: dominance, influence, steadiness, and conscientiousness) when I was working as an administrative assistant for a university, surrounded by others who were highly skilled as organizers and managers. The test was offered to us to highlight our strengths, and my results were literally the opposite of everyone else in the room. They all excelled in being analytical and ordered, and all of my skills were about feelings and needing freedom. At the time I felt embarrassed, as if I was missing a chip to be an effective worker, but the process led to my boss asking me to teach, which was already my undergrad degree and previous experience, helping me to get back on track with what I did best.

The two most popular personality tests are probably Myers-Briggs and Enneagram, both of which are helpful in identifying strengths and weaknesses and also just validating who we are as human beings. There is a lot of debate about whether we put too much faith in these tests, and most professionals, even the people who are trained to administer these tests, will admit that they were never meant to completely define us. They are much more useful in helping us consider ourselves and others and understand that not everyone experiences the world the way we do.

Finding out that I am most closely aligned with INFP (introversion, intuition, feeling, perception, often described as the mediator) on the Myers-Briggs scale didn't really tell me anything I didn't know about myself; it just made me feel more comfortable in my skin and accepting in how I experience life. Acknowledging that I am a 2 on the Enneagram (helper, caregiver) was similar in that I could see myself more clearly, acknowledging my strengths and also how I can deteriorate if I don't feel like I'm being recognized for helping (my shadow side). The goal is less about defining ourselves and more about finding a healthy way to utilize our skills and stay clear about our motivations.

Knowing that my husband is a 3 on the Enneagram (achiever) allows us to work better as partners, providing us language for why our versions of success (mine is about relationships, while his is more financial) didn't always match up. Balancing these versions of success gave us a better foundation when it came to our work, and our conflicts were fewer because we knew our desired outcomes were usually different. We debated less about who was inherently right and wrong and focused more on how to speak up for our needs and respect each other's perspective.

This practice is so helpful when it comes to parenting because although our children are still growing into themselves and developing their personalities, they are most likely quite different from us in the way they experience the world. Our point of view may be so different from our children that we feel as if we are failing or, worse, feel offended by the way they live. But respecting that there are many different ways to be a human not only frees you but also frees your children. Backing up and watching how they live allows us to pull from their strengths rather than force our will. If we notice that our children do better if things are written down rather than spoken, then we make that a priority. If we find that they need time by themselves in the morning or time to connect before bed, we do our best to honor what they need.

You don't have to give your kids a personality test or label them with an Enneagram number (these tests are usually recommended for adults because kids are still in the process of developing), but you can begin to notice their strengths and weaknesses and can listen when they talk about what interests them the most.

**You can share your point of view while staying open to the fact that some of what you share and teach will be**

helpful and supportive, and some of it may not fit who they are or where they are currently. There are many ways to be a person, and your kids need some room to figure themselves out.

One test that can be helpful for all ages is understanding your "love language" and the love languages of the people you live with. Author Dr. Gary Chapman recognized five different ways of expressing and receiving love while working as a marriage and family counselor: words of affirmation, quality time, receiving gifts, acts of service, and physical touch. We may appreciate all five, but there is usually one that becomes our true "love language." Not everyone communicates love in the same way, and people have different ways they prefer to receive love, which means if we want our loved ones to feel our love, we should figure out the language they speak.

My love language is most definitely words, but my husband tends to show love through acts of service. If my phone or computer has an issue, he's on it, and if I need a ride somewhere or I have a problem to solve, he's all in. But I've had to ask him for words when it comes to encouragement or even praise for the work I do or something less significant like getting dressed up for the night. In turn, I have learned that the words and praise I tend to heap on him don't really make that big of an impact and that he feels my love most when I show up for him when he's in need.

Our oldest daughter is a blend of acts of service and physical touch, and my middle daughter is much more focused on words and is not as interested in physical touch. Our youngest daughter is definitely quality time and physical touch, and she appreciates full attention when doing one-on-one activities. Taking a phone call or being distracted by texts are more hurtful to her than her sisters. These realizations allow us to talk about our needs and how we can best support each other, keeping us away from the mindset that we should all think alike. We don't, and the belief that what hurts or doesn't hurt you applies to everybody else will challenge our most important relationships. The Golden Rule of "treat other people the way you want to be treated" has been revised to "treat other people the way *they* want to be treated," necessitating some attention and curiosity to what we need and how we show up for the ones we love.

## For You

* Practice speaking up about what you really need rather than pretending you don't need anything or that it's someone else's job to know what you need.

* Practice speaking with clarity, but not dominance. Be thoughtful about how you share your opinion and allow others to offer their perspective.

* Consider the words you choose and why you choose them. Recognize when your words are

hurtful or harmful, and speak up when others use harmful or disparaging language in your presence.

* Become an active listener and really hear what your children have to say. Offer them eye contact and a calm presence, reflect back what they say to you, and take a deep breath before you respond.

* Consider taking a personality or love-language test to figure out your strengths and weaknesses and share what you learn with the ones you communicate with the most.

## For Your Kids

* Allow your children to share their perspective without judgment. Even if you don't agree, you can honor their willingness to speak up and share.

* Help your children find a balance between sharing their opinion and needing to win or be right. Listen to what they say and respect their perspective, and then share how you feel without needing to win or be right. Engage them in recognizing that thinking differently has benefits and that we don't need to agree on everything to get along.

* Talk to your kids about the words they choose and why they choose them. Discuss why and how swear words are used (they can have a place) and how cruel words can be used to devalue or dehumanize.

* Remind your children that while speaking up for themselves is important, listening is also a vital communication skill because it allows others to feel heard, understood, and connected.

* Recognize that your child's learning and interests may be different from yours, and support them in appreciating what comes naturally. Be curious about your child's natural skills and allow them to teach and share what they love.

## Chakra Six

# THE RIGHT TO SEE

*Experiencing Our Senses and Intuition*

Third-eye center

## INDIGO

Practice listening to your intuition, your inner voice; ask questions; be curious; see what you see; hear what you hear; and then act upon what you know to be true. These intuitive powers were given to your soul at birth.

**—CLARISSA PINKOLA ESTÉS,**
**Women Who Run with the Wolves:**
**Myths and Stories of the Wild Woman Archetype**

## Inner Knowing

The sixth chakra, often called "the third eye," is about clear seeing and the ability to visualize, imagine, and hold a greater vision for life. Most of our life experiences are viewed through our five senses, but we all have a "knowing," what some call a "sixth sense" or intuitive sense, about what's right and wrong for us. It's really just a question of whether we're willing to acknowledge and honor what we know.

Sixth-chakra development is often connected to spiritual awakening. It can happen anytime in life, but I tend to notice it in my clients between the ages of thirty-five and fifty-five. It's commonly referred to as a midlife crisis, but it's just as easily described as a shedding of the false self and a desire for something more meaningful and real. It's like a return to the teenage years, where we reject parts of ourselves and society that no longer fit so we can begin to embody who we really are. In Erik Erikson's stages of development, identity versus role confusion is the adolescent's dominant concern, and the journey of the midlife adult, often due to the experience of becoming a parent, can kick-start this stage once again. Or the adult may be venturing into a desire to offer something more, similar to the eighth stage of Erikson's theory, generativity versus stagnation, which usually happens between the ages of forty and sixty-five. This stage is typically about experiencing a need to create or nurture things that will be here after we are gone, through mentoring or creating positive change to benefit others.

Regardless of the motivation, it results in a willingness to look to ourselves instead of the outside world in an effort to trust and follow our own inner knowing. Before modern technology, we had to rely on signals from the environment and a more primal instinct to guide us, just like birds can sense when a tsunami might hit or squirrels know when it's time to gather food for the winter. Humans also have these intuitive sensibilities, but we are so clouded by our world experiences and inundated by other people's opinions and expectations, it makes it much more difficult to trust in what we feel and know.

People who have easier access to their intuitive abilities, like psychics, clairvoyants, mediums, or highly creatives, will say that all people have the ability to utilize their more intuitive selves, but it necessitates practice and a willingness to strengthen the muscle over time. I have experienced what I call "downloads," bursts of ideas or information through pictures or outlines that I can see in my mind. While I am much more open to these bursts of information, historically, I would push them away with great skepticism.

When I was unwilling to listen to my own internal guidance, it usually led to increasing anxiety and eventually physical challenges. In my twenties, I was moving full speed ahead and not listening to anything my mind or body was saying. I kept fainting (at work, at bars, walking down the street), which landed me in the emergency room, and one doctor predicted I had multiple sclerosis. The choices I was making at the time weren't overtly horrible, but they were wrong for me. I moved at a frantic pace so I wouldn't have to feel or acknowledge this truth, and my body wouldn't allow me to continue. I quit my job, went back to school, went through a breakup, and managed to somehow get back in alignment over the course of a year.

What was true for me wasn't necessarily true for the people around me, and I disappointed, or at least surprised, a lot of people when I halted my career, found a new apartment by myself, and took out a significant school loan to become a social worker. It seemed as if I was disrupting my life in every way, but the fainting stopped, and I felt like I belonged in my body again.

Trusting and exercising our muscle of intuition is an ongoing practice, and a version of this fainting story has happened other times in my life, thankfully with shorter lag times and fewer medical issues. Sometimes doing what's best for us means we have to do really hard things, like unintentionally hurt someone we love or disrupt our surroundings. This is painful no matter what, but it becomes even more painful if we fight against it or ignore what we know to be right.

So many of my clients tell me they know the right answer but are too scared to do what they know. They come to me hoping I will confirm that they don't have to do anything or that I have a different answer. The job of a therapist is less about providing answers and more about helping people in becoming more self-trusting and autonomous. It's about supporting them in integrating what they know while accepting what may seem difficult or contrary to the outside world's opinion. I think about Anna Quindlen's 2000 commencement speech at Villanova when she said, "The voices of conformity speak so loudly out there. Don't listen. People will tell you what you ought to think and how you ought to feel. They will tell you what to read and how to live. They will urge you to take jobs that they themselves loathe, and to follow safe paths that they themselves find tedious."

I think about this when a client tells me that they know what they want to do, but their parents, spouse, or employer tells them differently. I think about it every time it feels easier to do what's conventional or expected instead of opening ourselves up for scrutiny or criticism. But with enough experience, we learn that taking the conventional way can end up being even more painful. Others may feel relieved or satisfied with our decisions, but that's only because it serves their needs. If we choose to separate from ourselves and detach from what we feel, we inevitably face each day uncomfortable in our skin. Ignoring our inner knowing has its own set of consequences, and so much of our learning comes from the pain of overriding or not trusting what we know.

This is definitely true when it comes to parenting, especially because there are so many books and experts telling us what we should be doing and why there is only one way. I ironically write about parenting and have an office filled with parenting books, but I don't always love them. The idea that someone understands and has a final answer to your personal experience is too convenient, and while I know our society loves final answers and most experts are doing their best to help, there are too many variables to insist that there is one way. Effective decision making necessitates knowing yourself, knowing your child, and being present with the moment.

The best scenario is that books offer some clarity and empowerment, but there is plenty of room for parents to do what they know intuitively. Using a structured and rigid approach might work in our jobs, but it's not applicable when we are talking about raising human beings. We have to take so many things into account, including mood, time of day, our child's personality and learning style, and a hundred other issues that have to do with what it means to be a person.

**Sometimes the only thing that makes sense is deviating from the structured plan and doing what's right in the moment, especially if it's about offering more compassion, giving more hugs, listening more intently, or taking a breath before doing the next thing.** We have to loosen our grip on the *right* way and pay more attention to the *right way right now* if we want to stay connected to ourselves and our children.

## Truth

Stephen Colbert described the word *truthiness* on *The Colbert Report* in 2005 by saying, "I don't like books. They are all fact and no heart."[1] At the time I laughed, not knowing how "truthiness" and fact denial would invade our culture through the next decade.

The understanding of truth has gotten so muddled, especially in politics and the self-help community, that it's difficult to discuss without feeling angry, offended, or defensive. We force truth into a binary—I'm right and you're wrong—without understanding the nuance of experience, perspective, and motivation. We can respect both science and spirituality without disparaging or disregarding either, but we are blocked by our need for certainty and desire to win. We lessen our humanity in an effort to be right; we disregard our internal compass to maintain the upper hand.

I have watched peers, and even former teachers whom I've respected, argue with epidemiologists and experts who have dedicated their lives to studying disease. I continue to watch leaders disregard the science around climate change as we watch hurricanes, fires, and other natural disasters destroy our cities and lives. I watch women tell their stories of trauma and assault and read gaslighting tweets calling them liars and manipulators. In disbelief, I watched people storm our nation's Capitol believing this somehow demonstrated love of country.

I believe love wins, and I value personal truth and individual expression—but for love to win, we need to stay grounded in reality while maintaining empathy for others. Personal truth is fundamental, but it can never encapsulate the whole of all experiences. Truth is not choosing a side and then digging in; it's finding the space between education and our essential humanity.

In Adam Grant's book *Think Again*, he writes that neuroscientists have found that when our core beliefs are challenged, it triggers our primitive "lizard" brain, causing us to move into fight or flight and behave irrationally. Our ability to take a breath and practice "confident humility," the realization that we don't know everything but we do have the capacity to learn, is how we stay open to learning and growth. Saying "I don't know" doesn't mean we are insecure or ignorant, but rather it means that we have the courage to listen and ask questions. It's impossible to learn if we can't even admit that we have something to learn.

I study cults and cultlike teachers because, unfortunately, I've had many cultlike experiences. As a lifelong seeker, I have had spiritual teachers who insist I follow and study with only them, yoga teachers who insist they have the only path to enlightenment, and other practitioners who have claimed that only they know what's best for me. I have felt the initial security and comfort of having access to "truth" and then the eventual pain and disillusionment that come from realizing how power, sex, money, or greed plays a role in accessing "truth." These have been traumatic experiences that have broken my heart and wounded my spirit, but over time they have also strengthened my sense of self and discernment. I still have teachers, body workers, and spiritual advisers whom I admire and learn from, but they are not people who ask for allegiance or worship. They offer expertise and care and then trust me to choose.

Cults and cultlike teachers have an attractiveness that continues to make perfect sense; it can be so intoxicating to find a person or group who says they have all the answers, to believe that if we just do certain things, we are guaranteed greatness while others are not. This speaks to our need to belong and also our need to feel powerful and be considered good while others remain bad. I have seen this with people who are invested in well-known cults and in political ideology and conspiracy theories as well as people who are obsessed with a specific teacher or guru. I have also seen this with people who believe their religion is the only way, with some of my students who are current or former gang members, with friends who are obsessed with the new celebrity eating plan, and with clients who have an abusive or narcissistic partner.

The bottom-line belief is that this person or group will somehow give us something we don't have, that we will be made right or worthy, and that others will be made wrong or less than. Exploiting vulnerability to gain control or using dark psychological techniques to stoke fear and shape thinking is destructive. Anyone who says their way is the only way or that they have all the answers doesn't, and as French author and Nobel Prize winner André Gide said, "Believe those who are seeking the truth. Doubt those who find it."[2]

I have reaped the benefits of positive psychology, mindfulness, yoga, interpersonal neurobiology, and other ways of understanding human behavior, but these industries also get hijacked by bad actors who have chosen the profession for only moneymaking rather than bettering lives. Supporting others with personal growth can be a noble way to make a living, but some veer off the path of helping and focus solely on power. They keep their business model intact by building an audience that is completely dependent on them and looks to them for guidance in every aspect of their lives. This ensures a continual stream of income while the work loses its essential center and purpose. It re-creates a parenting model where the child looks only to the parent for answers rather than learning to choose or live for themselves.

Columnist David Brooks explains this phenomenon through theologian Augustine's description of having our "loves out of order." He says that we all have different loves, like family, money, affection, status, and truth. We get into trouble when these loves get out of order, when we put money above family or status above truth. That's when we lose sight of our integrity and make choices that harm others and inevitably harm us.

I have had teachers who have told me they have all the answers and have learned later that their personal lives were filled with abuse or illegal acts. I have paid money to people who said I needed to invest significantly before they offered me any kind of support and then gained nothing in return. I saw the red flags but talked myself out of them, mostly because I still carry some childhood baggage that outside validation is essential, that teachers are like parental figures whom I want to please. I wanted them to tell me I was doing things correctly and that I was worthy.

Every negative experience has shown me what kind of teacher I need to choose and what kind of teacher I want to be. Healthy teachers act as helping hands along the way so people can reach out for help when needed. But their goal is to offer sturdiness and support in locating ourselves, not to make us accountable or dependent on them.

This is also a blueprint for parenting. If we show up for our kids without holding on too tightly or forcing them to need us, they can ask for help while trusting their own inner knowing. They can find truth in education and expertise and also monitor and respect their own personal awareness. They can realize they have always been enough, not because they are better than others, but because we are all having the same human experience. They can know that they don't have the answers for everybody, but they do have the power to choose for themselves.

The basic right of the sixth chakra is to find your own Truth, by seeking wisdom from your inner and outer worlds. This is a delicate balance, an ongoing practice of outside learning while simultaneously trusting what we feel. Religion, politics, and other social structures can cloud our own personal insight, so the goal of the third eye is to trust our own wisdom in the face of social pressure. The timeless truths like love, connection, dignity, and compassion are guiding forces when we are faced with uncertainty, and if any group or person is not respecting the inherent dignity of people or is more focused on hate than love, consider that a glaring red flag.

## Mindfulness

Everything in this book is about mindfulness, but chakra six is where we really break down its importance. By definition, mindfulness is the ability to pay attention to what's happening right now. It's the human ability to be fully present, aware of where we are and what we're doing, and not overly reactive or overwhelmed by what's going on around us. Every human being has the ability to be mindful, but it takes practice to access it when needed.

If we're walking through the woods, it's easiest to take the well-worn path. It's the path that's been cleared out and mowed down, making it easy to locate and utilize. Like driving home from work without thinking, we can walk this route on autopilot because we've done it a million times. It's the same with our brain when our neurons constantly fire in a particular configuration (remember that *neurons that fire together wire together*). A path is created that becomes well worn and practiced, and if we aren't paying attention, we easily slip into recurring patterns, feelings, or choices that are more representative of our past than our present.

Creating new neuropathways in our brain necessitates paying attention to the moment and choosing something new. This means we need to forge a new route, like walking through trees and brush in the forest that so far have been untouched. Because it's new, it may feel arduous and unpredictable; each step needs to be assessed with a perseverance and willingness to stay alert. That's not to stay in a state of hyperarousal, but an awake state that is paying attention to the moment rather than going back into autopilot.

Jazz improvisation is similar to mindfulness in that the musician is completely connected to the moment and the other musicians. With pop music and the more typical verse-chorus-bridge structure, we basically know what we are going to hear, but with jazz the next sound and where it goes next are unpredictable. Musician Miles Davis said, "When you hit a wrong note, it's the next note that you play that determines if it's good or bad."[3] This is a great way to look at how staying awake to our surroundings continues to offer us opportunities to try again, assess what's needed, and stay present to reality.

Understanding the importance and practice of mindfulness is our way through every storm. Every challenge I've had in my life has scared the shit out of me, mostly because I relate it to past pain, other people's stories, or the future unknown. The only thing that has allowed me to stay grounded and take a confident step forward is by staying in *my* story and *this* moment. I can have hopes and goals to chart the course, but what's more important are my present-moment decisions, my willingness to pay attention to the next right thing and appreciate even the most subtle, enjoyable experiences.

When my dad was chronically sick, when my mom was diagnosed with dementia, when I experienced miscarriages, when my children were struggling, and even in the midst of my own depression and anxiety, I was forced to practice staying in the moment instead of figuring out how it was all going to unfold. Sometimes walking into a room, asking a question, or making a choice had the potential to paralyze me if I allowed myself to get lost in thought, so I practiced breathing and then choosing, breathing and then moving, breathing and accepting that I could do only one thing at a time, forging new paths over and over again. I also practice this in less daunting experiences, like when I need to meet a writing deadline, teach a class, or meet with a new client. Instead of deciding how it's all going to work, I just do what I'm expected to do in that moment, and somehow things continue to move forward.

Some people connect mindfulness to spacing out, losing track of time, or overall procrastination, but I have found it to be quite the opposite. While I truly enjoy spacing out and letting go, mindfulness is more of a temporary respite rather than an escape from everyday living. Mindfulness is about paying attention to the next step so I can continue to move forward with a sense of freedom, actually getting more done because I know what needs to be accomplished, without a fear of doing it. My college roommates will tell you that I finished my term papers way before they were due, and my husband will tell you that my presentations and classes are completed days ahead of time. Mindfulness has allowed me to be on time rather than separate from time, moving forward in the moment to make sure things get done.

Author Elizabeth Gilbert said that her pragmatic mother taught her that "done is better than good" and that instead of being an idealist gripped with fear or inertia, we can take things as they come rather than use our energy to actively avoid.[4] This is true whether it comes to starting a necessary conversation, replying to a text, or saying something difficult to our kids or partner. Avoidance is not mindful; mindfulness means we are paying attention so we can show up and get things done. And while pragmatism and idealism are paradoxical and can often run headfirst into each other, I've found that a lot of times they work as a team. Similar to the head and heart, with the head keeping the list of what must be done and the heart staying in tune with what feels right in the moment.

There are so many books about the practice of mindfulness that it's worth everyone's time to investigate its history, benefits, and ability to offer a sense of clarity and intention. When I first started teaching mindfulness to college students more than a decade ago, most had never heard of it. But now it is mainstream, with the military, CEOs, and the entertainment industry utilizing and discussing its benefits with ease and normalcy. As a society, we now embrace the research and effectiveness of mindfulness, but we don't always utilize the practices in our own lives. My clients tend to say, "I know, I should totally do that . . ." but then trail off into the varied reasons they don't practice. To tease them I throw out this Zen proverb: "You should sit in meditation for twenty minutes every day—unless you're too busy. Then you should sit for an hour."[5]

## Meditation

Mindfulness and meditation are connected, but they aren't synonymous. Mindfulness is a quality or experience, and meditation is a practice or tool to develop mindfulness. Meditation acquaints us with our brain so we can learn how it works and strengthen our ability to appropriately handle everyday situations. It's like weightlifting to get stronger or practice runs toward an eventual marathon. Meditation allows us to hone the tools we need to be more mindful in everyday life.

Meditation may not initially feel good, or at least it didn't for me. Sitting down to meditate is like holding up a mirror to your brain—the racing thoughts, the feelings, the contradictory messages, the worries and lists. Meditation is not creating these things; it's revealing to you what is happening in your brain when you aren't paying attention. The brain is super noisy and busy, and noticing the noisy and busy is the first step toward an interesting meditation practice.

The objective of meditation is not to "turn off" your brain. Like the heart and the lungs, the brain is a processing machine that will always be "on" while we are alive.

The job of the brain is to take in the current environment, past experiences, future deliberations, and anything else it's exposed to and continually mull it over, so thinking is exactly what it's supposed to be doing. When people say they are "quieting" their brain during meditation, they aren't turning anything off; they just learn how to *watch* the thinking rather than get *caught up* in the thinking.

The brain is not always telling us the truth; sometimes it's just cycling through past experiences or browsing through anxiety-provoking future outcomes. Thinking about something doesn't mean we have to act on it; we can just notice that our brain is thinking and gently move on. We can't stop thoughts from coming, but we can get used to how our brain thinks and decipher what's helpful and what's harmful. As mindfulness teacher Jon Kabat-Zinn said, "You can't stop the waves, but you can learn to surf."[6]

Meditation helps you recognize when your brain is stuck in the past or future versus focusing on what's happening right now. The now, which is synonymous with mindfulness, is manageable, inhabitable, and usually comfortable. What's uncomfortable is recycling the past or worrying about the future, two places we can never be, because we can only be here. Meditation is a practice of learning to be here now even while our brain continues to process and churn.

Meditation is how we create space between ourselves and the mind so we can begin to pay attention to our body. Our brain is our primary message center, but messages are being sent from our bodies as well, messages we often miss because our thoughts are all encompassing. Our body, especially our heart, has a communication all its own. The heart is not anxious or overwhelmed; it's much more peaceful and trusting. If you are an adult, it's probably been broken a time or two (or twenty), but it somehow pieces itself back together with love. It beats to keep every aspect of the body working as a unified team, working as a true center as it sends blood and love to every organ. I have found that my favorite meditation practices are focused around the heart, my favorite being the loving-kindness meditation.

For the past twenty years my meditation practice has been imperfect but somewhat consistent, and I average around eleven minutes a day. I've tried all sorts of formal and informal types of meditation with many different teachers, and it's led to a mix of things that work for me. There is not one way to meditate; there are many ways and possibilities. If one method or teacher doesn't feel right, continue to research others. Find a book or teacher to get you started, but then, more important, just sit down and practice. Try not to get lost in the right way or the best way, and just sit and breathe.

I meditate in my bedroom near a window, in a comfy meditation chair my mother-in-law gave me for my forty-third birthday. I have a screen around the chair that helps separate me from the rest of the room, and I have a small bench, sometimes called an altar, with figures that have special meaning—like a small Buddha and Jizo Sama (or Ojizo-sama in Japanese honorific language) statues; elephant, lion, deer, and turtle figurines; and a small statue of Jesus in the lotus position, surrounded by animals. I have rocks, pictures, my grandmother's rosary beads, an angel made of clay, a compass, small art projects from my girls, and some *Wizard of Oz* memorabilia. I have a vision board that I change about once every six months and Post-it notes all over the window of thoughts or ideas that come to me before or after meditation.

I have stacks of journals that I write in, and for the past five years I've read the daily passage from Mark Nepo's *Book of Awakening*. I use essential oil and light two candles to begin and then blow them out when I'm done. I set a free meditation timer on my phone for eleven minutes and start paying attention to my breathing to calm and settle (see Chakra Four about breathing). I have different types of mantras, but I appreciate the loving-kindness meditation (sometimes called "metta") the most, because it focuses on sending yourself love and then sending the same love to family and people you may not even know, including people you don't like, which has its own degree of difficulty.

This small corner in my room is one of my most special places, and while it is set up for meditation, I am just as happy to sit there and read. Just being in the space is a grounding experience, so I offer the space to my girls if they ever need a safe place to sit. I consider it a sacred place, but not so sacred that I won't allow others to appreciate it. Some people don't need a specific space, like my husband, who prefers to just sit outside in a chair and meditate. One of the most special parts of meditation is finding a way to make it your own, to find a practice or tools that represent who you are. These things can change as you go—I have added and subtracted things from my space; I have pulled down all the Post-its and then started over. I have written in journals and then decided to not write for a few weeks. There is something fluid and intuitive about the whole experience, where instead of focusing on how others do something, we get to create how we want something to be.

Meditation is not about striving, competing, or yet another experience where you feel like you have to prove yourself. Meditation is personal and different every time we sit down, with some sessions feeling better or more useful than others. But every session is still worthwhile, and an important learning from meditation is the acceptance that no experience should or will feel the same. One of my favorite meditation analogies, first taught to me by the Reverend Ed Bacon, is the comparison to a snow globe. When we initially sit down to meditate, everything in our mind feels erratic and shaken up, just like the snow inside the glass. But as we sit, the snow gently settles to the bottom, allowing our body to relax. There are times that I finish meditation and my thoughts still seem erratic, but at least I am aware of them. A small amount of space has been created between me and my thoughts, and then I don't overact to everything I think.

I have my college students start by meditating only two minutes a day and then build up the time as they feel ready. I encourage them to sit up, not lie down so they don't fall asleep, and to use an app like Headspace or Calm or just try silence. Some people insist that meditation be as long as twenty minutes or an hour, and some swear by morning and evening meditation. The hope is to discover something consistent and sustaining, something that fits into your life and offers you something helpful or at least interesting.

Remember that a meditation practice is not the end; it's the workout so you are more capable of handling the everyday uncertainty of life. If you have practiced breathing through thoughts and emotions during meditation, you will be better able to do this during a difficult conversation with your spouse and kids. If you noticed during meditation that thoughts and feelings come and go, you may feel less anxious during the day when a fearful thought creeps in.

Meditation allows us to mind our mind, and our mind holds the power to perceive our reality. Our ability to calm or at least acknowledge our mental overreactions can make our world feel less threatening. To decrease our overreaction to a comment from our partner or kids, to lessen our annoyance at the driver who cuts us off in traffic, to perceive a challenge as an opportunity rather than a roadblock can literally alter our daily experience.

Noticing what we think and becoming more deliberate about our thoughts offers us a small window to choose: to recognize that we have the power to perceive, and that we are not at the mercy of an initial thought or old story, to ease some of our fear and anxiety and notice what we may need to work on but also what's already working. Meditation does not make everything in the world okay, but it offers awareness and strength to be okay in the midst of our challenges.

## Imagination

Adults tend to think that imagination is reserved for children or childlike experiences, but imagination is our capacity for innovative thinking and creative expression, a part of us that operates in images, symbols, myths, and stories. It's the part of childhood that we should hold on to and continue to practice, because it's the starting point for anything we want to bring into reality.

Ironically, the word *imaginary* is synonymous with being "unreal," and while some things are, indeed, not initially tangible, anything we want to create begins with the imaginative process. If we discount the visions of our imagination, we cut ourselves off from our creative impulses and limit the impact we can have on the world. There is a difference between imagining what could be and holding a false illusion about what is. An imaginative vision is a possibility, a goal to inspire us, something that moves us forward, while an illusion is a certainty that's forced into place, something we believe is real and unchangeable. An illusion is stuck, whereas a vision is fluid and open.

The best part of writing, music, communication, or any other creative endeavor is that you never know where you'll end up. You can allow your imagination to take you on a ride, with new ideas and experiences literally being pulled into existence. These are the moments I live for, when I'm at my computer or teaching or even if I'm in a conversation with my husband or kids. Imagination is seeing beyond what has already been and being open to something we can't yet fathom. New ways of thinking, being, performing, or interacting are always possible; there are limitless doors waiting to be opened.

After the 2016 election, in the midst of the pandemic and racial justice protests, and during health scares and other uncertain challenges, I found myself leaning on imagination because my typical tools and solutions no longer had the ability to alleviate my fear and discomfort. I literally had to surrender believing that I knew what to do and, instead, be open to what I did not yet understand. *Hope* and *faith* became my go-to words because I had to put my trust in something I could not yet see.

Instead of believing there was only one solution or that things had to be a certain way, it became clear that I had no idea how things should be or how things would shake out and that my individual point of view lacked the vastness of a greater perspective. Feeling lost and out of tricks allowed me to be in the moment with less certainty and more openness, with less have-tos and more what-ifs. Holding a new vision for what can be is not a waste of time; it's a necessity for our ever-evolving survival.

We all grew up witnessing the concerns and problems of earlier generations, and we inevitably learn that responsibility is a high priority. We learn that responsible adults need to be serious and pay attention, forcing us to constantly strive to survive rather than live and enjoy life. Daydreaming and spacing out are considered a waste of time for adults, and lying on our backs in the backyard wondering what can be is considered procrastination. But our fear of irresponsibility and failing at life can lead to a lack of imagination about what we want to create in life. Instead of considering the endless possibilities for our human time on earth, we focus solely on being serious and responsible in an effort to have nothing happen to us. But as Dory says to Marlin in the midst of his worry about Nemo, "You can't never let anything happen to him. Then nothing would ever happen to him."

My mom always tells a story about how my dad would sit in his chair and stare out the back window while she would be busy doing housework. When she would ask him to help, he would say, "I'm sitting here planning our future." We always laugh because I'm quite sure my dad was avoiding what my mom was asking him to do, but I also believe that he was daydreaming and imagining what was possible, seeing something in his mind that was not yet a reality. *The Thinker* statue always lived on the corner of my dad's desk, because he always believed that contemplation was essential for good decision making. That statue now sits on my desk, and life has definitely taught me that **dedicating time to imagining what we want to create is far from irresponsible. Slowing down to contemplate what could be is what allows us to take responsible steps forward, to recognize what we want to do rather than show up as who we've been told to be.**

When children dream and tell you that they want to be a professional ball player or the president of the United States, you don't need to declare the odds of this happening. Their imagination is taking them to a place that makes them feel capable and powerful, a place that can motivate them during dark times or empower them when they need to make decisions. Not all of these children will become athletes or politicians, but their ability to envision what's possible for themselves gives them the drive to move forward in often unpredictable ways. The original goal may not be the end result, but the energy from the imagination keeps them moving forward, creating and renewing rather than giving up when they don't get what they want.

It shouldn't be mandatory for us to lose our childlike thinking once we have reached adulthood. As adults we need it more than ever. One of the things I love most about my husband is his joy of play through games and sports and his desire to create games and competition to keep people connected. It is completely possible, and some would say necessary, to appreciate a childlike imagination and the lighter side of life while remaining responsible for our adult lives.

When I was two years old, I was given a stuffed monkey—named Monkey—that still lives in a chair in my bedroom. I have gone through every life experience with Monkey, crying into his shoulder when I was sad and alone, hugging him when I got good news, and just feeling better because he sleeps close by. When I had the flu for several weeks a few years ago, Monkey laid next to me in bed because my kids and husband had to keep their distance. As a forty-nine-year-old woman, I still feel comforted by my stuffed animal—similar to the magic of Calvin and Hobbes, with Calvin and his tiger maintaining a relationship that lives in Calvin's imagination. The adults around Calvin have lost their ability to imagine, so when they see Hobbes they only see a stuffed tiger slumped next to the couch. But Calvin sees and experiences a sidekick and support system that allows him to maneuver and manage his days, a necessary companion so he can move through life less afraid.

Our imagination is about appreciating the unseen and our connection to what lives inside of us. We can call this our spiritual selves, our personal destiny, or just our more lighthearted nature. Pretending this part of ourselves is unnecessary or irresponsible denies our joy and blocks our limitless possibilities.

### For You

* Make it a habit to "listen" to what you hear and feel and become more trusting of your inner guidance. You can seek therapeutic or coaching support if this process feels inaccessible or daunting.

* Trust your own truth, but always leave room for expertise and new information. Seek the balance between feeling what's right for you and learning more.

* Practice noticing the moment through slowing down and breathing. Notice how you race through the day or move through the day on autopilot, and take steps to pay better attention to now.

* Create a meditation practice that works in your life. It can be two minutes a day or thirty minutes twice a day, but make sure it's doable in your current situation. Take a class or find books to support you as you learn.

* Respect imagination in your house by playing with your kids and listening to their stories and by finding ways to nurture your own imaginative processes throughout the day.

## For Your Kids

* Build your child's self-trust by allowing them to choose things that impact their day-to-day life, like their clothes, room decor, or haircut. Give them space to tell you what feels right to them rather than telling them how or what they should feel.

* Discuss the difference between self-trust and expertise and how the best decisions are based on a mixture of both. Support them in tapping into their internal knowing by placing a hand over

their heart before they make decisions or by journaling about what they feel.

* Talk to your kids about mindfulness and what it
  means to be present versus focused on the past
  or future. Help them practice breathing before
  they speak or choose, and remind them that while
  their brain gets anxious about old and new things,
  right now, in the moment, they are safe.

* Introduce your children to meditation and how
  sitting in silence for a few minutes a day can
  change the way our brain sees the world and processes information. Help them set up a mediation
  space and support them in finding phone apps
  (like Headspace and Calm) to make it easier.

* Allow imagination to live far beyond childhood.
  Let them keep their stuffed animals and toys as
  long as they want so they can hold on to parts of
  themselves that make them feel safe and more
  creative.

.....................................

# THE RIGHT TO KNOW

*Connecting to Something*
*Greater than Ourselves*

Top of head

## VIOLET

> And it now occurred to me that maybe the whole point
> was, in fact, to lose yourself. But not in the sense of
> confusion—in the sense of connection to something
> bigger than yourself. . . . Getting lost to be found.
>
> —TANUJA DESAI HIDIER, Born Confused

## Enlightenment

While the root, or first, chakra, connects us to the earth,
the crown chakra is our connection to the universe. The
crown, or seventh, chakra, is at the top of the head and
is represented as the color violet or white. In Sanskrit it's

called the *Sahasrara*, the "thousandfold" chakra, since it is pictured as a lotus having a thousand white petals.

This is the chakra of humanity, the realization that we are connected to something larger. We are a piece of a big puzzle, a drop in an infinite ocean. This is conscious awareness, the understanding that we are part of something greater than ourselves.

This sounds lofty, but it can actually be quite subtle. One of the greatest misunderstandings about this consciousness, often referred to as "enlightenment," is that once felt, it sticks around. While a select few claim to be in a heightened state of enlightenment at all times, the vast majority of humans have momentary glimpses of enlightenment throughout their lives, a flash of heightened awareness that is fleeting.

It can happen during or after childbirth or while sitting with someone who is sick or dying. It can happen when we fall in love or when we have deep gratitude for someone who helped us while we were in deep despair. It can happen in nature, while walking through a forest or looking at the ocean, or while taking care of animals or plants. It can also happen during meditation or yoga or any other exercise focused on stillness or going inward.

It is difficult to hold this feeling of enlightenment, but most can remember the experience of it. It's hard to explain, and once we begin talking about feelings of universal connection, words fail the experience. Actor Jim Carrey explained this by saying, "One day I woke up and I was everything and I was everyone, I was no longer a fragment of the universe, I was the universe. And ever since that day, I've been trying to get back there. . . . [I]t comes and it goes, it's like riding a wave, sometimes I'm on and sometimes I'm off, but at least I know where I want to go."[1]

The quote "Before enlightenment, chop wood, carry water. After enlightenment, chop wood, carry water" is an appropriate explanation of the enlightenment experience. Feeling the connection to something beyond ourselves can alter our perspective, relieve our anxiety, uplift our sense of self—it's an internal experience that allows us to live in the world with greater compassion. But we can never escape being human, and even with the feeling or experience of enlightenment, we still continue to live our daily lives of work, responsibility, and challenge.

The experience of enlightenment doesn't make us different or special; it actually shows us that we are all one and the same. A glimpse of this universal connection can relieve our egos, if only for a moment, and allow us to witness each other with new and compassionate eyes. Enlightenment uplifts our thinking and grounds our sense of self, allowing us to feel part of the whole rather than separate. It helps us to respect our place in the world and honor the dignity and worthiness of others.

We begin to notice that even the word *enlightenment* is yet another thing that people want to have, get, and then hold. The word becomes a distraction, just another thing we are trying to achieve rather than experience. As psychologist John Welwood wrote:

> *Forget about enlightenment.*
> *Sit down where you are*
> *And listen to the wind singing in*
> *your veins.*[2]

Enlightenment is not a putting on of wisdom; it's a feeling and understanding that we are a piece of the oneness of life, that we can trust where we are and trust what lives beyond our minds. We can notice the workings of the world and how even in chaos things somehow, paradoxically, fit together.

## Interconnectivity

Understanding interconnection can be understood neurobiologically or metaphysically—in the way we are hardwired or in the way we experience ourselves and each other. It's the foundation for understanding human beings and our interdependence on each other.

Our interconnectivity was made abundantly clear during the pandemic. Never before had we realized how intertwining and overlapping our lives could be and that while we may love to draw borders and separate ourselves from other nations, there are challenges that we will inevitably share.

But instead of understanding our interconnected nature, we tended to sort ourselves based on ideology and politics, turning against each other in an effort to demonstrate our rightness or need to "win." There are many reasons for this polarization, but a core issue is fear—our fear of being vulnerable with each other, our fear of getting hurt, and, ironically, our fear of disconnection.

It's a human connectivity crisis, and the solution is understanding how much we need each other and why we need to reinvest in each other. Our interconnection is innate, but our belief in this connection is constantly tested and undermined. When we believe there is something greater at stake—think natural disasters, the pandemic, family crisis—we become willing to ask for and accept help regardless of race, culture, or political leanings. I remember reading about the Texas hurricane in 2019 and how when boats arrived to save people from their homes, nobody was asking the helpers or the stranded who they voted for or what church they attended. They just became human beings accepting and offering help. This is what humans do; this is how our programming works.

Interconnection starts with our sense of belonging, the feeling that we are an essential part of a group and connected to something bigger than ourselves. In the book *The Happiness Hypothesis: Finding Modern Truth in Ancient Wisdom,* Jonathan Haidt calls this "vital engagement," building relationships and a sense of community where we know we are valued and needed. Being around others doesn't guarantee a sense of belonging; it's our ability to feel accepted for who we are and engage in meaningful interactions that leads to connection.

Family is the first place where we can experience this sense of belonging and connection, or it becomes our first experience with lack of belonging and disconnection. As parents we have the power to establish a foundational sense of belonging by honoring all aspects of our children, especially in the ways in which they differ from us.

This type of acceptance and belonging is fundamental to all humans, a type of connection that is less of a want and more of a need. A 2020 Massachusetts Institute of Technology study found we crave connection and interaction in the same region of our brains where we crave food, and a 2005 study showed that social exclusion and physical pain are experienced in the same region of the brain.[3]

In her book *Braving the Wilderness*, Brené Brown writes about the definition of true belonging as "the spiritual practice of believing in and belonging to yourself so deeply that you can share your most authentic self with the world and find sacredness in both being a part of something and standing alone in the wilderness. True belonging does not require you to change who you are; it requires you to be who you are."[4]

It can feel counterintuitive, but our belief in the inextricable human connection offers us a structure to be ourselves and show up as we are. We can stand up for what we believe, regardless of the pushback and criticism, and we can trust that we are deeply connected to others and the world in a way that can't be undone. We can understand that we are here because we are needed and necessary and that who we are, even if different, is what the world needs.

When we don't recognize our connection to the whole, we may cling to groups or beliefs that stifle our sense of self by keeping us quiet and restrained. Instead of listening to our inner knowing, we listen to what others demand because we are afraid of being wrong, cast out, judged, or not loved. Some people in power deliberately provoke this kind of divisiveness for their own political advantage, polarizing different groups so they fight with each other. This creates a distraction that allows powerful people to stay in power.

To solve our problems, we must debunk the polarizations, name-calling, and blaming so we can recognize we are on the same team, seeking similar outcomes. We breathe the same air and collectively suffer from the disruption of earth's climate, and to survive we have to recognize our common humanity and work together to solve global problems.

To make progress, we can expose and reject the fears that keep people apart. Many of our nation's problems—climate, racism, nuclear weapons, the unjust criminal justice system—are rooted in fear. It's fear that makes us beholden to the opinions of others, the threats from politicians, and the constant trappings of the media.

Our trust in interconnectedness is what allows us to be vulnerable, get uncomfortable, and learn how to be present with people without sacrificing ourselves. Trusting who we are is what allows us to play our sacred role, to follow our hearts instead of the crowd, to show up with love instead of fear, to find strength in our diversity rather than believe we should all be the same.

## Sacred and Scared

After meditation I often write a word on my hand with a Sharpie to focus on something helpful throughout the day, and one morning while attempting to write the word *sacred*, I flipped the letters *A* and *C* and wrote the word *scared*.

I thought about it all day, how similar these words are, with only one letter moving between them, and how different they are when it comes to how we see and experience the world. *Sacred* is about honor and respect, about seeing every moment, person, and thing around us as worthy. *Scared* is about fear that none of this is true, that safety is elusive, that we are alone and must hold on for dear life.

Being scared is similar to doubt, yet doubt is in, its own way, sacred. Doubt is what allows us to compare our insides to the outside world, to figure out what works for us and what doesn't ring true. I once heard someone say that doubt is *divine tough love*—an indicator that we are growing up and into ourselves, that we have a sense of belonging and capacity to find our place and relate to the world.

Doubt is a willingness to be curious, to investigate further and be open to new information. One thing we can always depend on is change, and to be open to change we must be willing to doubt what we once knew so we can be open to what comes next. Chuck Yeager, former US Air Force officer and the first pilot to have exceeded the speed of sound, was quoted as saying, "Just before you break through the sound barrier, the cockpit shakes the most."[5]

Doubt is a cockpit shaker. It is highly uncomfortable and scary to reconsider what we once thought was true. But the uncomfortable shaking precedes the breakthrough, the ability to see ourselves and others with more clarity. Once we move through the shaking and break through to a new place, we find ourselves with a more expanded point of view, a way to see and understand things in a new way. This isn't a onetime occurrence; we are given many opportunities to doubt and relearn throughout our lifetimes, with the same level of discomfort but more trust and willingness to be transformed.

Recognizing the similarity between scared and sacred has allowed me to be more thoughtful about my fear, to allow it to rise up rather than believe I need to push it down. I've made more room for fear and doubt because they seem to be messengers, acknowledgers of things I might have missed or parts of myself that are seeking some attention or comfort.

Being scared is never comfortable, and it's difficult to rest or be calm when our cockpit is shaking incessantly, but we can learn to express it, investigate it, and allow it because we know that something bigger may be uncovered within the discomfort. We begin to unwind things we may have learned or been told and gain access to our more sacred selves, the part of ourselves that knows life is always unfolding, never static.

## Devotion

Devotion is where the process of all of this learning comes full circle. My *Ray of Light* experience described in the Prologue was a realization that I didn't yet have my arms around what I believed or what I wanted to teach my children. Devotion was the willingness to venture down the path of self-exploration and to continue to make it a priority and practice.

Devotion is not an intellectual understanding but a dedication to the experience of showing up and learning, of successes and missteps. It's about paying attention and remembering that self-exploration is about fits and starts; it's never linear. In a similar way, author Barbara Brown Taylor observed that life is less like a train with arrival times and final stops and more like a sailboat navigating the weather and water. Sailing, like life, is an adventure: we set out with an intention, and we come back with a story. The trip may be shorter or longer than expected, and we never know what we will see, what we will experience, or who we will become.

We can't always decide what we will learn or what direction we will go, and our lives cannot be perfectly mapped. Obstacles, and even some of our best experiences, are inevitably unpredictable. Our commitment to devote time daily to meditation, journaling, prayer, movement, communication, and observation is the strength training required to manage the instability and unpredictability while we are on the water.

In 1943 Abraham Maslow proposed a psychology theory of human motivation called the *hierarchy of needs* that presents human needs in the shape of a pyramid in ascending order. Our basic needs, like physiology and safety, were at the bottom, and our more high-level, intangible needs, like love, esteem, and self-actualization, were at the top.

It may appear that a person can move to higher-level needs only once their basic needs are adequately fulfilled, and this makes absolute sense, in that eating, sleeping, and shelter are necessary to survive. But it's also true that the ability to pay attention to our higher-level needs, like love of self or others, can alter our behavior and shift our ability to access our more basic needs.

Self-actualization does not need to wait until every aspect of our lives is in place; we can practice self-understanding and self-appreciation even in the midst of crisis, not to demonstrate our spiritual fortitude or dedication, but to gather strength and understanding to make it through. Too many people say they will meditate when they have more time or sleep or eat better when a project is done, disregarding why these practices are important in the first place.

Self-understanding is similar to self-compassion in that it's necessary in every aspect of our lives. Paying attention to how we relate to ourselves and talk to others can decrease our missteps and smooth out our most basic day-to-day experiences.

We may also need to move in and out of our devotional practices, letting go when they start to get stale. A decade ago, when I was studying to become a yoga teacher, I proudly told my teacher how I hadn't missed a day of practice in more than a year and how devoted I was to my mat. She smiled and said, "Maybe your next practice should be skipping practice for a day or two."

There have been times when my meditation practice became monotonous or just unproductive, so I let go and found something new. Or I just let go and watched a lot of Netflix. I am just as devoted to taking breaks as I am to maintaining continuity.

At some point, I find myself easing back into devotional practices, like finding comfort in a book or journal writing. I rediscover the power of a healthy devotion and gain a heightened enjoyment, mostly because I was willing to take a break.

We have to be careful to not make devotion into superstition, where we believe our lives are functioning in a certain way because we are adhering tightly to a list of things we must do. It's okay to miss a day of yoga; it's okay to miss a day of meditation. Not only is it okay, but it may be necessary as well. The periods of time where I put away my books and let go of self-awareness studies led to experiences I may not have had otherwise. These experiences ended up deepening my more typical devotion practices when I eventually picked them up again.

Devotion is not about doing the same thing over and over in a demonstration of allegiance or a method proving we are special, enlightened, or committed. Devotion is much more fluid, a willingness to pay attention to what's needed in the moment. Being able to hear our inner needs is our connection to something greater. Our willingness to flow with change is devotion to ourselves; it's the unpredictability of our sailboat journey.

Being comfortable with change and unpredictability sets the stage for how we raise our kids. Instead of trying to move them through linear steps with the promise of something greater each step of the way, we allow them to experience the typical back-and-forth in every stage of their lives. We normalize the challenges and develop an appreciation for them because they build the resilience our kids need to live a good life. We encourage our children to listen to their inner knowing, to trust who they are, to feel capable in navigating rough winds but also take in the beautiful sunsets.

We can't predict how our children's lives will go. Even if we are privileged enough to offer them a head start through education and opportunity, we can't guarantee that their experience will be what we dreamed. And the truth is their lives should not take shape the way we have dreamed, because their lives should follow *their* patterns and choices; their sailboat ride should be their own.

Parenting is the greatest opportunity to see ourselves as we are, to have a mirror held up to us so we know the truth. Knowing that our children are watching us can feel like pressure, but it's also permission to ensure that we are devoted to our own self-awareness and well-being. Parenting is less about what we say and much more about how we show up. To be devoted to ourselves is to be devoted to our partners, our children, and the world as a whole.

Devotion is our desire for something bigger. My clients, my students, and my daughters all tell me they want to connect with something meaningful and real, to really know themselves and live from this place of integrity. They want to know God or understand the universe; they want to know why they are here. These are life's ultimate questions, and it's only human to be devoted to searching for the answers. Through the search we discover that the questions are a lifelong study, that we live and dance inside the questions throughout our existence.

My hope for each of us, especially my children, is that we trust this process. That we can manage the waves of life, the difficult questions, the trying times, to remember that the discomfort and challenges we experience do not make us less than but make us human.

Devotion is recognizing that this is our one life, that we have an internal knowing about who we are, and that we have limited time to decide if we are going to truly show up and live as that person. Devotion is loving your people so much that you are willing to do the hard work so you can be in better relationship with them and be what you are asking them to be in real time.

Devotion is work, and it's also a relief. It's feeling the grief of letting go in an effort to find something truer. Devotion is reflection, a willingness to check ourselves on a moment-to-moment basis, to realize that living from a place of meaning isn't an intellectual decision but a daily practice.

*For You*

* Discuss or journal about experiences where you felt one with nature or the universe and begin to notice how often you experience a glimpse of enlightenment.

* Notice the ways in which we depend on each other, how our society requires different skills and thinking to function and run. Practice being grateful for your doctor, your server, an engineer, an artist, or a friend who supports you and allows you to thrive.

* Recognize that some of our scariest experiences or deepest fears are the best pathways to sacred awareness. Instead of running from scary moments, take time to investigate what you are feeling and why.

* Have devotional practices that set the tone for your day and ground your sense of being. Be willing to take breaks and find new things, remembering that even devotion needs space to grow and change.

*For Your Kids*

* Offer your children plenty of experiences in nature, specifically stars, insects, animals, and trees, so they begin to notice and feel the power and sacredness of our surroundings.

* Talk with your children about how other people's skills and talents allow our society to function. Help them develop a gratitude practice for those who share and serve. Point out the people who design the roads, build them, and then maintain them so we can drive places. Point out the farmers who grow the food, the people who transport it, and those who sell it so we can buy it at the grocery store. Do this with every aspect of society to demonstrate that we need each other's skills and contributions to survive.

* Talk to your kids about fear and allow them to speak about what scares them. Instead of telling them to not be afraid, allow them to share and remind them that being scared is human and a messenger of what's most important (security, relationships, connection, belonging).

* Introduce your kids to devotional practices, such as journaling, meditating, dancing, yoga, singing, or painting, and then allow them to pick and choose what works for them at any given time.

# CONCLUSION

What lives at the heart of Zen Parenting is the ability to sit bravely in the discomfort of change and look unflinchingly at how we relate in order to make our relationships more connected and our world more compassionate. It's a unique experience with many moving parts, so calling it a technique or parenting style doesn't fit. It's too personal and ever changing; it's more of an individualized approach to paying attention to ourselves and the world, a willingness to stay present with what's happening and engage in life as it is.

The majority of our stories about life are created in childhood, with some of those stories propelling us forward and offering a stable foundation and some of them keeping us stuck and afraid, with an unwillingness to trust ourselves or connect with others. Our lives become a mixture of both, holding tight to what sustains us and dismantling what no longer works.

Relationships are alive, always growing and changing. We have to learn how to move with this change, and instead of pushing against it we can accept that relationships are fluid and new expectations are often required. I was my dad's daughter for a long time; he was my safety net and source of expertise. When he got sick when I was twenty-seven, my sister and I became his safety net, and we became daughters to our dad.

He was chronically ill for almost seventeen years, and for the vast majority of that time, he didn't want to talk about it. He was an eternal optimist bordering on denial, and besides giving us updates about feeling good or having a good checkup, discussing his struggles with congenital heart disease was rare or nonexistent.

This had its upsides in that my dad always focused on the good and never wanted us to be burdened by him. But it was also a burden that while we could always share love and gratitude for each other, we could not state the obvious. I remember when a hospice worker came to his room to sing and play the guitar, I was so worried that she would introduce herself as an end-of-life caregiver and my dad would be forced to confront the truth of the moment. When she was done playing, he just thanked her and proceeded to tell us all that he had decided to start lifting weights again to regain his strength.

My dad had a strong mind and a failing body. Our family had an unspoken agreement to disregard what we knew about his body so we could stay in touch with his mind. My dad's dignity was based on this agreement, so as his daughter I honored it. He did not start lifting weights again; he died only a few days after the hospice worker sang for him.

My mom has a strong body and a failing mind. She was diagnosed with dementia recently, but my sister and I knew that her mind was changing several years ago. It was difficult to differentiate her grief over losing my dad and an actual dementia diagnosis, but, eventually, it became obvious. Then my sister and I went from having a mom to becoming our mom's daughters.

Caring for my mom is the flip side of what we experienced with our dad, and I can't say that one is better than the other. They are just what they are, and we do the best we can to stay in the moment with what's happening. We show up for what is; we stay in relationship with the person who is right there in front of us.

Zen Parenting is about staying in relationship with ourselves and the ones we love. Instead of thinking there is a right way to be with people, we trust there is a right way to be with this person in this moment. It's realizing that three kids, all with the same parents and raised in the same house, will grow up to be completely different humans. It's about knowing that one day we can be overwhelmed with work and social obligations on our calendar, and the next day we are experiencing a quarantine and an empty calendar due to a global pandemic.

Self-awareness is not about always getting things right; it's about paying attention when it goes wrong and staying open to why. Personal growth is never about a destination or linear learning; it's about the willingness to ride the waves of emotion and trust that we have the tools necessary to keep our heads above the water.

Taking care of ourselves means we can't go it alone; we need to ask for help when we struggle and be humble enough to learn from those who are older and younger. We can't control our lives and the people around us, but we do get to choose our choices. We get to decide how to be in this moment, how to show up for someone we love, how to question something that no longer works, how to break down and have a much-needed cry.

The lack of hard-and-fast rules in life understandably makes life feel uncertain. The truth is that we have never had certainty; we just thought we did. Our greatest and most difficult lessons come from things we thought were certain, like money, a job, a home, or a relationship. When we lose one of them, we have to grapple with the fact that our belief in guarantees was unsound.

While certainty is elusive, we can focus on things that keep us grounded, no matter the circumstance—grounding forces such as self-awareness, compassion, connection, and mindfulness, things that are always available during calm, crisis, or change. We can be self-aware enough to take responsibility for our actions and acknowledge and care for our needs, and we can offer ourselves and others grace and compassion. We can trust that connection is what stabilizes us and offers us hope and that we can stay mindful enough to focus on just this moment, rather than giving all of our headspace to past regrets or future worries.

Raising our children with these grounding forces will not keep them from pain and challenge, but it will offer them tools to deal with pain and challenge. These are the keys to being human, and as parents it's our job to role model how to use these keys. Pretending that life success can be found in a grade, a college, a job, or a partner is an untruth our kids will eventually figure out. They may get all of these things and more, but they will also inevitably experience disappointment and pain. They need to know that things don't always work out the way we planned, but there is always a way to navigate even the most difficult terrain.

But first, *we* need to know this. We need to begin this journey and have the willingness to pay attention to now, our past, and our experiences, both light and dark. When we trust that we belong and are connected to something greater, we not only get to enjoy and appreciate this understanding, but also get to live this way and know that our children will learn from our behavior.

A teacher once told me that we all evolve at different times, that self-awareness is not a race or a competition to specialness. The person who you believe is completely unevolved may turn a corner tomorrow; the person who seems to have it all together may hit a wall next week. We are all progressing at different rates, learning things in different ways.

Charles Bukowski's poem titled "Mind and Heart" is a reminder of what to remember:

> *read*
> *what I've written*
> *then*
> *forget it all.*

> *drink from the well*
> *of yourself*
> *and begin*
> *again.*[1]

I am blessed that I get to share what I know and love with you, but in the end this journey is yours alone. You get to drink from the well of yourself and trust in your ability to keep going in this uncertain world. You get to share yourself and what you have learned with the ones you love most. This is what keeps us alive and well, the ability to be in alignment with ourselves and love our people from this sacred place.

# ACKNOWLEDGMENTS

Everything my dad experienced was the "best" because that's how he wanted to experience it, and my mom was the first to tell me that obstacles might be gifts to help keep us safe. My parents shared a glass-half-full view of the world during difficult times, and they also shared a drawer full of personal growth cassettes (Wayne Dyer, Stephen Covey, Brian Tracy) that became fixtures in my tape deck.

My sister led the way and let me follow her around from high school to college to Chicago, so I always had a path until I found my own. My aunt has cheered for me since I was born, so there was always someone telling me I was enough. I have brilliant and beautiful friends who have supported me through decades of my life, becoming family and role models for my girls. Relationships are why we are here, and my people have kept me compassionate and optimistic, offering a sturdy foundation so I could study and write about what is painful and difficult.

Thanks to those who have listened to *Zen Parenting Radio* over the past ten years and to those who have attended a Zen Parenting Conference. Thanks to my social work students, clients, and women's circle. Everything makes more sense when we are learning together.

Thank goodness for Rea Frey, a writer whom I met in the green room at WGN Radio when we were booked as guests. Years later I asked her to edit my book, and she guided me through every stage of publishing, including introducing me to my agent, Rachel Beck, who always gives me the confidence to keep going when I'm losing faith. Thanks to Dan Ambrosio for bringing *Zen Parenting* to life and to the entire Hachette team for making me feel seen and valued.

Thanks to the writers who made me love writing: Anna Quindlen, Dani Shapiro, Cheryl Strayed, Gwendolyn Brooks, Mary Oliver, Mary Pipher, Brené Brown, Maya Angelou, Mark Nepo, Joy Harjo, and Anne Morrow Lindbergh. I read your work again and again. I feel what you say; I study the words you choose.

Todd, Jacey, Camryn, and Skylar: Whenever you ask me to name my favorite movie, I always say *The Wizard of Oz*. When I was very young, I felt what it was trying to teach, and I've spent the majority of my life trying to find the words to explain what I felt. This means I talk and write a lot, so thank you for being patient listeners and readers. My greatest hope is that you honor your feelings and find your words. Trust in what Glinda said to Dorothy: *"Home is a place we all must find, child. It's not just a place where you eat or sleep. Home is knowing. Knowing your mind, knowing your heart, knowing your courage. If we know ourselves, we're always home, anywhere."*

# APPENDIX

The books I return to again and again:

*The Gifts of Imperfection: Let Go of Who You Think
You're Supposed to Be and Embrace Who You Are,*
BY BRENÉ BROWN

All of Brené Brown's books have impacted how I understand the human experience, but this book encapsulates how to *unlearn what we have learned* and find our true selves in the process. This is the book I have used most frequently with my college students, and the list of ten guideposts are essential understanding on the path to personal growth.

*Differently Wired: Raising an Exceptional Child
in a Conventional World,*
BY DEBORAH REBER

While Reber writes about her own experiences with her twice-exceptional son, her book is vital to all parents in supporting our children for who they are rather than who we believe they should become. Her book (and friendship) has given me the strength and encouragement to support my kids in finding their own paths rather than caving to outside expectations and unquestioned conformity.

### *Peace Is Every Step:*
### *The Path of Mindfulness in Everyday Life,*
#### BY THICH NHAT HANH

This is the book I most commonly give as a gift due to its beauty and simplicity. The message and writing are simple, but far from easy, with this world-renowned Zen master asking us to practice mindfulness during the most difficult and mundane times. Suggesting a complete paradigm shift, he encourages us to see ourselves as each other or, as he describes it, *inter-are.* It's a deceptively subtle book relaying the most arduous message—wake up, wake up, wake up.

### *Gift from the Sea,*
#### BY ANNE MORROW LINDBERGH

This personal reflection helped me understand the joy and pain of motherhood and that I wasn't alone in feeling uncertain and conflicted. I read this book every year to remember that some advice is timeless and that, as a woman, I am never alone on this journey of balancing caregiving and personal freedom.

## Caste: The Origins of Our Discontents,
### BY ISABEL WILKERSON

Isabel Wilkerson's book provides the history of human rankings and power, sharing the stories of real people to better understand how the caste system has guided, and continues to guide, our politics and culture. There are so many important books to be read when it comes to race, inequality, and power, but this award-winning book was the most impactful because of its unflinching honesty and hope for common humanity.

## Eastern Body, Western Mind: Psychology and the Chakra System as a Path to the Self,
### BY ANODEA JUDITH

I bought this book around the time my second daughter was born, and I've returned to it again and again to navigate the understanding of the chakra system and how it intersects with psychology and wellness. This book uses the structure of the chakra system to map out individual development and is a deep dive into personal challenges and healing.

## *When Things Fall Apart:*
## *Heart Advice for Difficult Times,*
### BY PEMA CHÖDRÖN

When life hurts, I listen to Pema's audiobook as a reminder that falling apart and coming back together are the natural rhythms of life and that my ability to accept is how I find peace. Pema also explains that feeling fear means getting closer to an inherent truth and that running away from suffering is like running away from being alive. This book reminds us that being human means experiencing pain, but that the experience of pain has the power to develop compassion for ourselves and others.

## *Parenting from the Inside Out:*
## *How a Deeper Self-Understanding*
## *Can Help You Raise Children Who Thrive,*
### BY DR. DANIEL J. SIEGEL AND MARY HARTZELL

I use all of Dr. Siegel's books to better understand interpersonal neurobiology and how to better utilize the brain, and this book uses this research to explain how our childhood experiences shape the way we parent. It challenges us to better understand our own life stories so we better communicate with our children about the life stories they are creating. This book is the essence of our *Zen Parenting Radio* tagline, "The best predictor of a child's well-being is a parent's self-understanding."

## *Emotional Agility: Get Unstuck, Embrace Change, and Thrive in Work and Life,*
### BY SUSAN DAVID

My favorite books are about emotional intelligence, and the language and perspective of this book have been the most helpful, personally and professionally. Not only do we need to respect and honor the messages of our emotions, but we also need to practice agility and self-acceptance in how we respond to what we are feeling. Our ability to navigate our inner world is what determines our ability to adapt and find meaning in our lives.

## *A Short Guide to a Happy Life* and *Being Perfect,*
### BY ANNA QUINDLEN

Both of these little books sit on my desk as reminders that what others perceive as success may not feel good to us and what feels good to us may not be understood by others. They give me permission to live my one precious life and remind me that beauty and a sense of self are found in daily and ordinary things.

# NOTES

## Prologue

1. Lao Tzu, *The Tao Te Ching of Lao Tzu*, trans. Brian Browne Walker (New York: St. Martin's Press, 1995), 1.

2. Robert Rosenbaum, *Zen and the Heart of Psychotherapy* (New York: Routledge, 1999), 31.

3. Quoted in David Chadwick, *To Shine One Corner of the World: Moments with Shunryu Suzuki* (New York: Broadway Books, 2001), 3.

4. Mary Oliver, "The Summer Day," in *New and Selected Poems*, vol. 1 (Boston: Beacon Press, 1992), lines 18–19.

5. "Rumi: Quotes: Quotable Quote," Goodreads, www.goodreads.com /quotes.

6. Frank Ostaseski and Rachel Naomi Remen, *The Five Invitations* (New York: Flatiron Books, 2017), 1.

7. Sue Monk Kidd, *The Dance of the Dissident Daughter: A Woman's Journey from Christian Traditions to the Sacred Feminine* (San Francisco: Harper-Collins, 2016), 30.

## Introduction

1. Ijeoma Oluo, *So You Want to Talk About Race* (New York: Seal Press, 2020), 224.

2. "Mandela: Quotes: Quotable Quote," Goodreads, www.goodreads .com/quotes.

3. Mark Duplass, "The Power of Paradox," interview with Brené Brown, *Unlocking Us with Brené Brown*, podcast, May 13, 2020, https://brenebrown .com/podcast/brene-with-jay-duplass-and-mark-duplass-on-the-power -of-paradox.

4. Isabel Wilkerson, *Caste: The Origins of Our Discontents* (New York: Random House, 2020), 86.

5. Quoted in Heather Greenwood Davis, "Talking to Kids About Race," *National Geographic*, June 1, 2020, www.nationalgeographic.com/family /article/talking-about-race.

6. Quoted in Davis, "Talking to Kids About Race."

7. Shereen Marisol Meraji, "'Hispanic,' 'Latino,' Or 'Latinx'? Survey Says . . . ," *Code Switch* (blog), August 11, 2020, www.npr.org/sections /codeswitch/2020/08/11/901398248/hispanic-latino-or-latinx-survey-says.

8. Bryan Stevenson, "'Do Some Uncomfortable and Inconvenient Things': A Civil Rights Champion's Call to Action for CEOs," *Fortune*, June 27, 2018, https://laptrinhx.com/do-some-uncomfortable-and-incon venient-things-a-civil-rights-champion-s-call-to-action-for-ceos-2326241316/.

9. Austin Channing Brown, *I'm Still Here: Black Dignity in a World Made for Whiteness* (New York: Convergent Books, 2018), 173.

10. Erin Pahlke, Rebecca S. Bigler, and Marie-Anne Suizzo, "Relations Between Colorblind Socialization and Children's Racial Bias: Evidence from European American Mothers and Their Preschool Children," *Child Development* 83, no. 4 (2012): 1164–1179, https://doi.org /10.1111/j.1467-8624.2012.01770.x.

11. Brigitte Vittrup and George W. Holden, "Exploring the Impact of Educational Television and Parent-Child Discussions on Children's Racial Attitudes," *Analyses of Social Issues and Public Policy* 11, no. 1 (2011): 82–104, https://doi.org/10.1111/j.1530-2415.2010.01223.x.

12. Daniel J. Siegel and Tina Payne Bryson, *The Whole-Brain Child: 12 Revolutionary Strategies to Nurture Your Child's Developing Mind* (New York: Bantam, 2012), 69; Donald Hebb quoted in Richard P. Cooper et al., "Associative (Not Hebbian) Learning and the Mirror Neuron System," *Neuroscience Letters* 540 (April 12, 2013): 28–36, https://doi.org/10.1016 /j.neulet.2012.10.002.

13. Maeva Bonjour and Ineke van der Vlugt, *Comprehensive Sexuality Education: Knowledge File* (Utrech, Netherlands: Rutgers International, 2018), www.rutgers.international/sites/rutgersorg/files/PDF/knowledge files/20181218_knowledge%20file_CSE.pdf.

14. Bonnie Rough, *Beyond Birds & Bees: Bringing Home a New Message to Our Kids About Sex, Love, and Equality* (New York: Seal Press, 2018), chap. 4.

15. "Talking About Sex and Puberty," Focus on the Family, January 1, 2007, www.focusonthefamily.com/parenting/talking-about-sex-and-puberty.

16. Amie M. Ashcraft and Pamela J. Murray, "Talking to Parents About Adolescent Sexuality," *Pediatric Clinics of North America* 64, no. 2 (2017): 305, https://doi.org/10.1016/j.pcl.2016.11.002.

17. Walt Whitman, "Song of Myself," Poetry Foundation, www.poetry foundation.org/poems/45477/song-of-myself-1892-version.

18. Patricia Hill Collins, *Black Sexual Politics: African Americans, Gender, and the New Racism* (New York, Routledge, 2004).

19. Lin Bian, Sarah-Jane Leslie, and Andrei Cimpian, "Gender Stereotypes About Intellectual Ability Emerge Early and Influence Children's Interests," *Science* 355, no. 6323 (2017): 389–391, https://doi.org/10.1126/science.aah6524; Seth Stephens-Davidowitz, "Google, Tell Me. Is My Son a Genius?," *New York Times*, January 18, 2014, www.nytimes.com/2014/01/19/opinion/sunday/google-tell-me-is-my-son-a-genius.html.

20. Courtney Connley, "Women's Labor Force Participation Rate Hit a 33-Year Low in January According to New Analysis," CNBC, February 8, 2021, www.cnbc.com/2021/02/08/womens-labor-force-participation-rate-hit-33-year-low-in-january-2021.html; Megan Leonhardt, "9.8 Million Working Mothers in the U.S. Are Suffering from Burnout," CNBC, December 3, 2020, www.cnbc.com/2020/12/03/millions-of-working-mothers-in-the-us-are-suffering-from-burnout.html.

21. Stephens-Davidowitz, "Google, Tell Me"; Mary Pipher, *Reviving Ophelia: Helping You to Understand and Cope with Your Teenage Daughter* (New York: Riverhead Books, 2005), 37.

22. Soraya Chemaly, *Rage Becomes Her: The Power of Women's Anger* (New York: Atria Books, 2018), 8.

23. Gemma Hartley, *Fed Up: Emotional Labor, Women, and the Way Forward* (New York: HarperOne, 2018), 118.

24. "Gender Differences in the Economic and Social Impact of the COVID-19 Pandemic," WIA Report, July 8, 2020, www.wiareport.com/2020/07/gender-differences-in-the-economic-and-social-impact-of-the-covid-19-pandemic/.

25. Brené Brown, "The Courage to Be Vulnerable," interview with Krista Tippett, *On Being*, NPR, November 22, 2012, https://onbeing.org/programs/brene-brown-the-courage-to-be-vulnerable-jan2015/#audio.

26. David A. Cotter, Joan M. Hermsen, and Reeve Vanneman, "Brief: Back on Track? The Stall and Rebound in Support for Women's New Roles in Work and Politics, 1977–2012," Council on Contemporary Families, July 30, 2014,

https://contemporaryfamilies.org/gender-revolution-rebound-brief-back -on-track.

27. Brigid Schulte, *Overwhelmed: Work, Love, and Play When No One Has the Time* (New York: Picador, 2015), 170.

28. *The Mask You Live In*, dir. Jennifer Siebel Newsome (Representation Project, 2015), https://themaskyoulivein.vhx.tv/checkout/the-mask -you-live-in-feature-film.

29. Robert W. Blum et al., "It Begins at 10: How Gender Expectations Shape Early Adolescence Around the World," *Journal of Adolescent Health* 61, no. 4, supp. (2017): S3–S4, https://doi.org/10.1016/j.jadohealth.2017 .07.009.

30. Debora L. Spar, "Good Fellows: Men's Role & Reason in the Fight for Gender Equality," *Daedalus* (Winter 2020): 222–235, www.amacad.org /publication/good-fellows-mens-role-reason-fight-gender-equality.

31. "Major Depression," National Institute of Mental Health, last updated February 2019, www.nimh.nih.gov/health/statistics/major-depression .shtml; "Any Anxiety Disorder," National Institute of Mental Health, last updated November 2017, www.nimh.nih.gov/health/statistics/any -anxiety-disorder.shtml#part_155096.

32. "Suicide Prevention," Centers for Disease Control and Prevention, last updated March 23, 2021, www.cdc.gov/suicide/facts/index.html.

33. Glennon Doyle, *Carry On, Warrior: The Power of Embracing Your Messy, Beautiful Life* (New York: Scribner, 2014), 27.

## Using the Chakra System

1. Quoted in "Pioneers in Our Field: Jean Piaget—Champion of Children's Ideas," Scholastic, www.scholastic.com/teachers/articles/teaching -content/pioneers-our-field-jean-piaget-champion-childrens-ideas.

## Chakra One

1. Quoted in "Finding Freedom with Food: A Q&A with Geneen Roth," Kripalu Center for Yoga & Health, https://kripalu.org/resources /finding-freedom-food-qa-geneen-roth.

2. Bessel A. van der Kolk, *The Body Keeps the Score: Brain, Mind, and Body in the Healing of Trauma* (New York: Penguin, 2015), 91.

3. Van der Kolk, *Body Keeps the Score*, 102.

4. Centers for Disease Control and Prevention, *Preventing Adverse Childhood Experiences (ACEs): Leveraging the Best Available Evidence* (Atlanta: National Center for Injury Prevention and Control, 2019), 7, 8.

5. "Data and Statistics on Children's Mental Health," Centers for Disease Control and Prevention, last updated June 15, 2020, www.cdc.gov /childrensmentalhealth/data.html.

6. Anne Trafton, "Back-and-Forth Exchanges Boost Children's Brain Response to Language," *MIT News*, February 13, 2020, https://news.mit .edu/2018/conversation-boost-childrens-brain-response-language-0214.

7. "Albert Einstein: Quotes: Quotable Quote," Goodreads, www.good reads.com/quotes.

8. "Thinking Positively About Aging Extends Life More than Exercise and Not Smoking," *Yale News*, July 29, 2002, https://news.yale.edu /2002/07/29/thinking-positively-about-aging-extends-life-more-exercise -and-not-smoking.

9. Robyn Castellani, "Want to Change Your Life? Change Your Narrative. Here's How," *Forbes*, July 17, 2018, www.forbes.com/sites/break -the-future/2018/07/17/want-to-change-your-life-change-your-narrative -heres-how/?sh=5a1871dc1a9f.

10. Kelly McGonigal, *The Upside of Stress* (New York: Avery, 2017), 27.

## Chakra Two

1. Leslie Riopel, "Goleman and Other Key Names in Emotional Intelligence Research," Positive Psychology, January 9, 2020, https://positive psychology.com/emotional-intelligence-goleman-research.

2. Brené Brown, "The Power of Vulnerability," TEDxHouston, November 10, 2010, www.ted.com/talks/brene_brown_the_power_of_vulnerability.

3. Quoted in Anita Knight Kuhnley, *The Mister Rogers Effect: 7 Secrets to Bringing Out the Best in Yourself and Others from America's Beloved Neighbor* (Grand Rapids, MI: Baker Books, 2020), 59.

4. Elizabeth Gilbert, *Big Magic: Creative Living Beyond Fear* (New York: Penguin, 2016), 3.

5. Quoted in Sophia Ohja, "Reflection Quote 005: Emerson on Being Yourself," *Reflection Pond* (blog), March 9, 2018, www.reflectionpond.com /blog.

6. Brené Brown, "Daring Greatly," interview with Oprah Winfrey, *Super Soul Sunday*, March 17, 2013, www.oprah.com/own-super-soul-sunday /oprah–brene-brown-daring-greatly.

7. Gilbert, *Big Magic*, 273.

8. Stuart Brown, "Play Doesn't End with Childhood: Why Adults Need Recess Too," interview with Sami Yenigun, *All Things Considered*, National Public Radio, August 6, 2014, www.npr.org.

9. Randy Pausch, *The Last Lecture* (New York: Hyperion, 2008), 52.

10. "Cultural Discrepancies in Teaching Consent and Learning Safe Sex Practices: Netherlands vs. America," *Kay's RCL Blog* (blog), February 14, 2020, https://sites.psu.edu/rclblogkay/2020/02/14/cultural -discrepancies-in-teaching-consent-and-learning-safe-sex-practices-nether lands-vs-america/comment-page-1.

11. Hanneke De Graaf, Ine Vanwesenbeeck, and Suzanne Meijer, "Educational Differences in Adolescents' Sexual Health: A Pervasive Phenomenon in a National Dutch Sample," *Journal of Sex Research* 52, no. 7 (2015): 747–757, https://doi.org/10.1080/00224499.2014.945111; World Health Organization European Region, "Health Behaviour in School-Aged Children (HBSC)," www.euro.who.int/en/health-topics/Life-stages/child-and -adolescent-health/children-and-adolescents-in-the-who-european-region /youth-friendly-services/health-behaviour-in-school-aged-children -hbsc2.-who-collaborative-cross-national-study-of-children-aged-1115; "The Netherlands Has Lowest Rate of Teenage Mothers in the EU," DutchNews.nl, December 11, 2017, www.dutchnews.nl/news/2017/12/the -netherlands-has-lowest-rate-of-teenage-mothers-in-the-eu.

12. American College of Obstetricians and Gynecologists Committee on Adolescent Health Care, "Comprehensive Sexuality Education," Committee Opinion 678 (November 2016), www.acog.org/clinical/clinical-guidance /committee-opinion/articles/2016/11/comprehensive-sexuality -education.

## Chakra Three

1. Oprah Winfrey, Stanford University commencement speech, June 15, 2008.

## Chakra Four

1. Divya Kannan and Heidi Levitt, "A Review of Client Self-Criticism in Psychotherapy," *Journal of Psychotherapy Integration* 23, no. 2 (2013): 166, https://doi.org/10.1037/a0032355; Theodore A. Powers et al. "The Effects of Self-Criticism and Self-Oriented Perfectionism on Goal Pursuit," *Personality and Social Psychology Bulletin* 37, no. 7 (2011), https://doi.org /10.1177/0146167211410246.

2. Quoted in Mary Elizabeth Williams, "Nora McInerny Rejects the Cult of Positivity That Demands We Get Over Grief: 'Bitch, How?,'" *Salon*, March 26, 2019, www.salon.com/2019/03/26/nora-mcinerny-rejects-the -cult-of-positivity-that-demands-we-get-over-grief-bitch-how.

## Chakra Five

1. Maya Angelou, *Oprah's Master Class*, January 16, 2011.

## Chakra Six

1. Stephen Colbert, *The Colbert Report*, October 17, 2005.

2. "André Gide: Quotes," Goodreads, www.goodreads.com/author /quotes/7617.Andr_Gide.

3. Quoted in Josh Jones, "Herbie Hancock Explains the Big Lesson He Learned from Miles Davis: Every Mistake in Music, as in Life, Is an Opportunity," *Open Culture*, April 5, 2018, www.openculture.com/2018/04 /herbie-hancock-explains-the-big-lesson-he-learned-from-miles-davis.html.

4. Elizabeth Gilbert, interview with Claire Zammit, "Unlocking Your Creativity," March 31, 2016, *Evolving Wisdom* (blog), https://evolving wisdom.com/blog/unlocking-your-creativity.

5. "Meditation Quote 3: 'You Should Sit in Meditation for Twenty Minutes Every Day—Unless You're Too Busy; Then You Should Sit for an Hour—Zen Proverb," *Daily Meditate*, April 11, 2014, https://dailymeditate .com/meditation-quote-3-you-should-sit-in-meditation-for-twenty-minutes -every-day-unless-youre-too-busy-then-you-should-sit-for-an-hour-zen -proverb.

6. Quoted in Kadri Haljas, "Mindfulness: You Can't Stop the Waves, but You Can Learn to Surf," Triumf Health, July 2, 2017, www.triumf.health /news/2017-07-mindfulness.

## Chakra Seven

1. Jim Carrey, "Jim Carrey on 'Awakening,'" interview with Eckhart Tolle at 2009 inaugural GATE event, *Eckhart Tolle TV*, originally aired on January 23, 2010.

2. John Welwood, "Mindful Poetry: 'Forget About Enlightenment,'" *Lotus Heart Mindfulness* (blog), June 12, 2019, https://lotusheartmindful ness.com/lotus-heart-blog/2019/5/28/forget-about-enlightenment.

3. Livia Tomova et al., "Acute Social Isolation Evokes Midbrain Craving Responses Similar to Hunger," *Nature Neuroscience* 23, no. 12 (2020): 1597–1605, https://doi.org/10.1038/s41593-020-00742-z; Geoff Macdonald and Mark R. Leary, "Why Does Social Exclusion Hurt? The Relationship Between Social and Physical Pain," *Psychological Bulletin* 131, no. 2 (2005): 202–223, https://doi.org/10.1037/0033-2909.131.2.202.

4. Brené Brown, *Braving the Wilderness: The True Quest for True Belonging and the Courage to Stand Alone* (New York: Random House, 2017), 157.

5. Quoted in Tuesday Ryan Hart, "The Shaky Cockpit," *The Outside* (blog), January 15, 2019, www.findtheoutside.com/blog/2019/1/15/the -shaky-cockpit.

## Conclusion

1. Charles Bukowski, "Mind and Heart," in *Come on In!* (New York: HarperCollins, 2009), 278.